JAMES'
STORY

ENDORSEMENTS

Exposed is a refreshingly honest and grace–filled book that captures the restorative work of God. James and Teri's story is a timely reminder of God's insatiable love for us even through our darkest moments.

CHARLES LEE
CEO of Ideation & Author of _Good Idea. Now What?_

Exposed is a true story of hope. As you read James and Teri's individual perspectives of their heart–wrenching trials, you will be moved and challenged. It's not every day you hear a comeback story of this magnitude. I am honored to call them my friends.

ANTONIO SABATO JR.
Celebrity Television & Movie Actor

James and Teri Craft are brave. Their timely book, _Exposed_, presents essential life lessons for each of us in a binocular view with both Teri and James disclosing the same account, yet with divergent compasses. Theirs is a story that illustrates the old adage: _You will either be ruled by the rudder or ruled by the rocks._ One was an expedition that led to repentance and the other, a courageous passage that led to forgiveness. They have navigated their past, but are not moored there. Rather, they have boldly chosen to set sail towards a bright future, for that is where the promises of God await.

DR. WAYNE CORDEIRO
Pastor & Author

You are in for a real adventure as you read through this book! James will share with you the amazing journey the Lord has taken him on...from the depths of hell to the heights of the Mount of Transfiguration.

More victories lie ahead for him, but through it all James has discovered that the shape of his soul is unique, that he has a special destiny here and now, and that behind the facade of our lives there is something sovereign, beautiful, and eternal happening. He is learning to see himself with the same delight, joy, and expectation with which God sees him every moment.

As a sexual addiction therapist, I walked through the Valley of the Shadow of Death with James and Teri. I listened as James screamed out in pain as he faced the fact of the insane addictive noose he had wrapped around his soul. I watched as Teri dealt with her issues as well; the effects of sexual bondage are not just a guy's problem, they are a family systems problem. I observed their souls at close range as they courageously and honestly faced the reality of their bondage. In the process, these two became a couple that I am incredibly proud of. There is no hype or denial any more; they are the real deal!

Yes, there is intensity, but it is the passion from two lonesome hearts that have finally found their way home to the Father. They have learned the passion of true intimacy, of the love that waits to take you home. Home where you are known and seen and where your life is treasured beyond every barrier of despair you have ever known.

So, enjoy! Hopefully, new insights of healing and wholeness will come to you as well in the process of walking with James and Teri.

DR. TED ROBERTS
Pastoral Sexual Addiction Professional
Founder of Pure Desire Ministries International

EXPOSED
A JOURNEY OF RENEWAL & HOPE

JAMES & TERI CRAFT

EXPOSED
A JOURNEY OF RENEWAL & HOPE
by James & Teri Craft

© 2015 by James & Teri Craft and Pure Desire Ministries International

ALL RIGHTS RESERVED

Published by:
Pure Desire Ministries International
www.puredesire.org | Gresham, Oregon | March 2015

ISBN: 978-0-9896598-5-7

JAMES' STORY **TABLE OF CONTENTS**

FOREWORD BY DR. JIM SCOTT

VICE PRESIDENT OF GLOBAL OPERATIONS;
DIRECTOR OF FOURSQUARE MISSIONS INT'L

James and I first met at a Foursquare Church youth camping week at Camp Cedar Crest in the San Bernardino Mountains in California. He was a cabin group leader just out of high school and the students loved him. In the words of the Book of Acts, I could see the grace of God on his life and ministry and it was obvious the hand of the Lord was with him as he served. I thought he was already moving into ministry leadership when I learned he would soon be leaving for my alma mater, Fresno State University, on a track scholarship and to earn a degree in geography with a minor in history. James was going to be a Bulldog sprinter!

Our friendship grew stronger, and it was wonderful to enjoy the blessing on his life and to see James' growing ministry responsibilities. Teri said "yes," and they were married. God gave them three amazing girls. As others saw James' gifts, new ministry opportunities were offered and accepted. He was hugely successful. His marriage and family were perfect. James' life was what so many ministers wanted and worked so hard to achieve. And then it all came crashing down on April 25, 2013.

I am James' friend and I was stunned by his failure. Our mutual friends were stunned as well. It was as if we all realized that we didn't know our friend and we didn't know what was going on in his life. For me there was no judgment, only deep sorrow and anguished prayers for the entire situation.

While I was stunned at my friend's failure, I was not surprised. I have been an "unknown" friend, a pretender, a compartmentalized man who self–medicated with pornography.

Today I am free, but as with James, my journey to freedom began many, many years ago by being exposed. For me, porn was a "pick–me–up" on a bad day and the reward for a good day. I once had the thought that pornography would be with me every day of my life. It's strange to reflect back and realize, I had no hope that I would ever be free and no will to live another way. As I healed, I learned that there were other deeper and more profound wounds in my life.

While our stories, sins, and failures are different, James and I share similar kinds of abuses while growing up and we both were sexualized by porn as preteens. James and I each became actors on our own stages and, as followers of Jesus who hoped to serve in the ministry, we knew the acting had to be top–notch. We acted to the audiences before us and we lived lies to such a degree that despair was always with us. There are deep core hurts that cry out to be healed!

I wonder how many people are participating in some type of accountability group or close community, but are only sharing just a part; only acting in a personal drama rather than being who they really are, sharing what is true for them and inviting others to love them as they are. Aren't we all longing to be loved unconditionally?

This book, *Exposed*, is an astonishingly courageous, transparent, and raw, yet redemptive, hopeful, and loving exploration by James and Teri of the storm that engulfed them. With the help of the Holy Spirit, each other, and the girls, their pastors, their church community, good friends, and imminently gifted and godly counselors, they learned important truths about their past, their faith, their thinking, their honesty, and their marriage and family. There is pain and promise on every page with sure help for those who are bound, yet long to be free.

As you read *Exposed*, I believe you, too, will be renewed in the joy that the Father continues to see the wayward son a long way off and runs to welcome him home. (cf. Luke 15:11–32)

The Father is looking for you and you can be free!

ACKNOWLEDGMENTS

*My Savior...*you pulled me out of my carnage and placed me on solid ground. You have never given up on me and have always walked beside me showing me the way home... thank you!

*Teri...*you are the love of my life. This is our love story, born out of ashes and despair. My heart is full of gratitude for your love and commitment to me, and I look forward to the journey that we have before us, where our love will grow deeper and stronger every step of the way. You are an incredible woman of God, and I'm excited to see how God uses you to touch this broken world with His healing hand. You are my love, my best friend...

*Rachel, Elise, and Grace...*I love you to the moon and back. You three are my shining stars, and I'm thankful to be called your daddy!

*Dr. Ted and my Pure Desire group...*you are my band of brothers.

INTRODUCTION

HEADLINE NEWS:

CELEBRITY COUPLE CALLS IT QUITS AFTER ALLEGED
ONGOING INFIDELITY AND PROMISCUITY.

SENATE HOPEFUL UNDER INVESTIGATION FOR ASSOCIATION
WITH HIGH–PRICED PROSTITUTE.

PASTOR OF LARGE CHURCH ADMITS TO AFFAIR AND IS
REMOVED FROM POSITION.

I was at the top of my game. I was a successful pastor at a large church with global influence, had the perfect family, and touted a spotless past. The harsh reality is that my whitewashed tomb was exposed for what it really was, and all that was hidden in the darkness was eventually brought to light.

Most people haven't experienced the public exposure of shame and had their deepest, darkest secrets revealed openly. What do you do when your sin is exposed for the world to see? What do you and your family do when your entire world crashes to the ground like a shattering glass house and people make quick judgments and bleak assessments? How do you deal with the losses? Who do you turn to for help and hope? Sadly, that final headline above exposed the issue in my life I most regret and the story my wife, Teri, and I will share in the pages of this book.

We feel compelled to share our story for two reasons. One is that 54% of pastors[1] and 64% of men[2] who will attend church this weekend are struggling with bondage associated with pornography. Our desire is that our story will give encouragement and hope to those who have wanted to change, but haven't had the tools to do so. Secondly, our prayer is for change in the church; in order to experience true revival and be a relevant hope to this and future generations, the church at large must wake up to the fact that we have to face this issue and provide help for those who are struggling. Putting my innermost thoughts and personal struggles in writing for all to see is way out of my comfort zone. But through freedom in Christ, I now dwell in a new and beautiful place of vulnerability and transparency with the Lord, my wife, my children, and those around me. It has become something of a new language for me, many long years in the making. I was terrified when asked if I would be willing to write what has transpired through my personal recovery and restoration as a testimony to help others. When many of the fearful thoughts and feelings of inadequacy I express in the following chapters bubbled to the surface, I felt my pulse quicken and my breathing shorten. *Tell my story…on paper…in a book… like the ones you find on a shelf in a store…for any and all to pick up to read and pass judgment on? You've got to be kidding.*

After a great deal of prayer and discussion with my loving family and those in my accountability circle, I realized that even

---

1 Brenton Evans, "Till porn do us part," FireProofMyMarriage.com http://fireproofmymarriage.com/dload.php?file=_images/_needhelp/InternetSafety.pdf (accessed Mar. 19, 2015).

2 Covenant Eyes, "Pornography Statistics: Annual Report 2015" http://www.covenanteyes.com/pornstats (accessed Mar. 19, 2015).

though this task was difficult and daunting, it was about more than me. Teri and I have heard countless stories of pastors, leaders, and public figures who've struggled in this area and had the damaging effects dismantle their lives. Yet very few ever talked openly about the story behind their pain, the path they took to get free, and the hope available to others who are in the same place. It's like everyone is waiting to see the *Where Are They Now* segment on TV, but nothing ever appears that gives even a glimpse that someone out there is making headway against this monumental issue. A conversation with a man in the Pure Desire men's group that I now lead pretty much says it all: "James, I would never wish what happened to you or your loved ones on anyone, but can I just say that I am glad you shared your story and are giving your life back to others who are struggling. If you wouldn't have given your testimony, I would still be in bondage with no hope. Thank you, my brother."

So here it goes! I invite you to come on a journey with us. As you can see, my wife and I have chosen to write this book together, with two different perspectives of a very difficult storm we faced individually and as a family. I will take you back to my childhood and walk you through the source of my personal pain and the place where I first began to develop a dysfunctional lifestyle. I will also walk you through the healing that took place as I got real and honest with what was driving my behavior. I will share special encounters with my Father in heaven.

I always loved Jesus and accepted Him into my heart as a small child, but when it came to accepting the love that God the Father had for me, I was unable to see through the lens of hurt and woundedness long enough to believe He actually could love someone as worthless as me. This created a shame–based filter for every thought and behavior in my personal life. Now, I see my

INTRODUCTION

Heavenly Father through health and freedom and have accepted His love for me. I have been able to forgive and love my earthly mother and father and embrace those situations that brought such pain and confusion as a child. I have allowed His healing touch to obliterate the walls I built around my heart and can hear His sweet voice give me direction for reprogramming my behavior.

I take full responsibility for the choices I made. I can't and won't blame others for those choices. I now understand the origins of my pain, but I also know the sin I allowed into my life brought great destruction upon many. I was once told that sin will take you further than you want to go, keep you longer than you want to stay, and cost you more than you want to pay. This, of course, is true for everyone who opens their life up to sin, but, regretfully, those sinful actions have the potential to hurt others, and the lasting effects can damage generations of precious people.

I ask for forgiveness, both for my actions and, by proxy, any actions that a person in leadership has made that may have hurt you in any time of your life. Through Christ there is forgiveness, hope, and the ultimate place of freedom that unleashes a profound relationship with our Heavenly Father who is faithful, unchanging, all–consuming, and the purest love.

On the flip side of this book, you will walk through this process from the perspective of the true writer in our family, my wife, Teri. You will see right away that God has given her a gift of communication with words. Remember, she had to deal with the ultimate act of betrayal that any wife could experience, and she beautifully explains how she clung to the Lord with every breath. She will guide you through a healing process that will revolutionize your mind and heart, and will do it in such a way that you'll feel you've just left the intimacy of our California living room.

Teri and I understand that reading about this journey will challenge you to the core of who you are. It will anger you, convict you, and encourage you. Our greatest desire is that what you read on these pages will lead you to the truth of who you are in Christ, who God created you to be, and who He wants you to reach with His love. Our prayer is that you will join with us in starting a grace–filled discussion with others regarding the issues we tackle. The very best way to expose the lies of the enemy is to bring the truth into the light. Come with us on this illuminating journey.

But you are the ones chosen by God, chosen for the high calling of priestly work, chosen to be a holy people, God's instruments to do his work and speak out for him, to tell others of the night–and–day difference he made for you—from nothing to something, from rejected to accepted.
1 Peter 2:9–10 (The Message)

Sincerely,
James Craft

Chapter 1
EXPOSED

No creature can hide from God.
Everything is uncovered and exposed for Him to see.
Hebrews 4:13 (GW)

On April 25th at about 11:15 a.m., I drove down the H1 toward Kalanianaole Highway, heading to our townhome. We had been living in Hawaii for four months in a town east of Honolulu called Hawaii Kai. Many people would say that Hawaii is paradise, and I would have to whole–heartedly agree. Not only is it one of the most beautiful places on the face of the earth, the Hawaiian people also are truly the kindest and most loving people we have encountered. For a surfer like me, this was truly paradise! I drove this stretch of highway every day from our residence, right on a water inlet that led to the open ocean, to New Hope Oahu, the church I served at on the west side of Honolulu. Coming from Southern California, driving in Hawaii took some getting used to. Where I was used to racing down the 101 freeway or the 405 at seventy–five or eighty miles per hour just to survive, I was now getting accustomed to a more peaceful pace of driving on a highway that had a speed limit of just 45 miles per hour.

On any typical day, this drive was refreshing for me. The drive home from church included such sights as Diamond Head on our right, along with stretches of crystal blue water with waves peeling off to one side or the other. We would know we were almost home when Koko Head, the great marker in our town of Hawaii Kai, would appear ahead in the distance. The reality, however, was that this was paradise lost.

On this April day, life as I knew it came crashing down. The heat and pressure of the volcano of lies that I spent so much of my time and energy trying to keep pushed down exploded in a violent eruption and everything disintegrated in one second. My life had been exposed. The lies and brokenness of my life were now uncovered for everyone to see, but that layer of exposure was just the surface of what my loving Father God needed and desired to do in my life. From my limited vantage point, all I could see was what was directly in front of me, not knowing a chain reaction of explosions, which had been in the making for the past thirty years of my life, had just been triggered. Being exposed were the deep woundedness, behavioral patterns, addictions, and the affair I had been involved in while living on the mainland.

At this point in my life, I didn't know which way was up or down, let alone forward. All I knew at this moment in time, on April 25th, was that this terrible lie I had wasted so much time and energy trying to cover up was now in the open; life as we knew it as a family was over and I was the cause. The feelings that flooded my body and the thoughts that rushed through my mind were uncontrollable. I didn't know where to go from here, other than home to confess to my wife, Teri.

Teri is the sweetest, most beautiful, loving, creative, God–fearing person I have ever known. We started dating our junior year in high school, attended youth group together, were voted

CHAPTER 1 – EXPOSED

Senior Sweethearts, and were even in the homecoming court together. We became best friends in those early years of our relationship, and were married July 11, 1992. In those almost twenty–one years of marriage, we experienced mountain–top events and deep–valley challenges that drew us together in many ways, but pulled us apart in other ways. Through it all we knew that we were meant for each other and that God perfectly united us here to fulfill His purpose through us as a team.

During those twenty–one years of marriage, God blessed us with three incredible girls, Rachel, Elise, and Grace, whom I love beyond words. I know you might be asking, "If you loved your family so much, how could you do such a thing?" I wrestled with this same question for months before this fateful day. As difficult as it is to understand, I couldn't put the pieces together in my mind regarding the progression of brokenness and the behaviors that came from that place of depravity. I had lived a lifetime of shame. The resulting sinful behavior, with which I had medicated the pain of my past, was eventually what my Heavenly Father exposed, unearthing the deep wounds in my life and systematically bringing healing and restoration, not only for me, but also for all willing hearts involved.

So, while I was driving down Kalanianaole Highway, my heart was collapsing in on itself. I knew that what I was about to reveal would likely destroy my marriage, hurt my loving wife and family beyond belief, and bring sadness and anger to those I was shepherding. I couldn't think about what was going to happen the next day or even the next month; all I could think of was how much damage I had caused and the reality that I couldn't escape anymore.

When I arrived home, it took everything I had to get out of the car. I remember the emotions that flooded my heart, and the fear of what was to come. Walking into the house, I called to see where Teri was. I heard her respond from upstairs in our bedroom. I walked upstairs, dread mounting with each and every step, not knowing what I was going to say, fear gripping my heart, shame and disappointment overwhelming my soul. I walked into our bedroom. Teri was on the other side of the room.

She saw that I was crying. She kept asking if the girls were okay, and if something happened to her mom. She started to panic, and then I came out with the horrible, but truthful words, "I've been unfaithful to you!" When those words spilled out, I saw all color drain from her face and shock fill her eyes. She then ran out of the room and out of the house.

At that moment, in my utterly crazy and unhealthy state of being, all I could think was what is going to happen next? I've come to understand after much healing and therapy with our dear friends and counselors, Dr. Ted and Diane Roberts from Pure Desire Ministries International, that I was so focused on me that I had little to no empathy for others. "Me" is how I had learned to survive since I was a young child, and those patterns led to a destructive end. Looking back, I understand clearly now that I was more broken and remorseful initially that I had been exposed, rather than having a heart of sincere repentance and sorrow for what I had done.

I imagine the hearts of some reading this might be feeling a wide range of emotions about that last statement, but I need to be transparent and honest with you because that is the depth of sickness I had reached. Yes, my heart broke for breaking my family's heart. Yes, I was angry at myself. Yes, I was sickened and shameful for living a double life with my family and the precious people in the church I served. But looking behind the mask of my life at that time, I was still trying to protect James. I will explain in more depth later in this book about that mask, but for now, I want to encourage you to keep reading no matter how angry you might feel. I pray you will open your heart to discover how the Lord healed my heart, mind, body, and spirit in such a way that empathy, compassion, and love were revealed and developed from the wreckage of what seemed like a worthless life. Please open your mind and heart to hear of one miraculous love story born out of the ashes of pain and loss that speak deeply of our Savior's ultimate love for all of us and how that love translated to everyone in our family. I am reminded of the words in Hebrews 4:13 (God's Word Translation):

No creature can hide from God. Everything is uncovered and exposed for him to see. We must answer to him.

God was not shocked or surprised by what took place that April day. He knew what was on the horizon, and faithfully guided us so that we would become all that He initially planned for us to be personally, as a married couple, and as a family. As a pastor, I'd get up every week and teach the Word of God to thousands of people, and those words were living and true and helped guide many to Jesus as their Savior. The very sad fact is that I didn't grasp in the deepest part of my soul the very words I was proclaiming. I'm not saying I didn't believe what God was saying through His Word, I just didn't believe, nor understand, the depth of God's love for ME.

It is in this area that I am convinced God wanted to do a double–sided exposure in my life. He wanted to expose the lie that I'd been living, but He also wanted to expose the lie that became a part of me during my childhood years. The Creator of the universe wanted me to finally comprehend His view of me, not the wounded, angry, and broken one that had become my false and deadly DNA.

We found out early on that this process was going to take a lot of work, warfare, and patience on my behalf and on behalf of those around me, especially my loving wife. Since it took over thirty years of life to get to where I was at that point, there was no way I was going to get out of this hole overnight. But through the power of the Holy Spirit, and support and direction from Dr. Ted and Diane, our pastors and friends Gary and Tammy Dunahoo, Pastor Wayne Cordeiro of New Hope Oahu in Honolulu, Hawaii, a handful of trusted friends, and my best friend and dear wife, God has raised me up out of that miry clay, and set my feet on the solid ground that I am so overwhelmingly grateful to live on today.

I know that this restorative process will ultimately take many years. While I'm here on earth, I will always have to deal with challenges that come my way. We are all charged to be aware of our weaknesses, but when I cling to my Father in openness and vulnerability, that is when I find ultimate healing and restoration, not only for me, but for generations to come. I know deep down in my soul that I cannot live any day of my life without God. He loves me, and it has taken about thirty years to be able to sing "Jesus Loves Me" and really get it. I know if I try to live one single second on my own, I will royally mess up, and leave a trail of carnage behind me.

In the chapters ahead, it is my desire to walk you through the process of how I got to that place in April 2013, and what the healing and recovery was like for my family and me. Walking through comprehensive and intentional healing and restoration, you find out how many layers of hurt and pain have been built upon each other throughout your life. When I thought I had made great progress, the Lord would lift up another layer and walk me through the next step. He faithfully did the same for my wife and our family as well. As wretched and shameful as I considered myself to be initially, I started to realize how wounded I had been growing up, and the only way I knew how to deal with that pain was to medicate it somehow. Instead of using drugs and alcohol, I chose to become a workaholic and started viewing pornography at a very young age. When my world seemed out of control or stressful from working to gain people's approval, porn was my way out. It was my fantasy world, which medicated the pain temporarily, but layered shame and hurt even deeper, so deep, in fact, that I could no longer access parts of my soul.

Think about it. I was a pastor for seventeen years of my life. People saw me and listened to me as I taught God's Word. I saw people healed, give their lives to Jesus, and fully serve Him. But I was trapped in a web of despair and lies. I believed I couldn't tell anyone what I was dealing with; every time I tried, I was shamed even further, and, in some cases, told to keep it to myself. I saw what other Christians had done to those spiritual leaders who struggled in life, and my web of lies, worthlessness, and shame grew deeper and deeper. So, I kept this compartment of my life hidden for most of my existence, leaving me and my loved ones open to the lure and destruction of the enemy's deadly plan.

I never allowed anyone to get close to me. It wasn't a fully cognitive plan; it was just my survival tool. All my friends were kept at arm's length. I'd learned early on to compartmentalize my life to the highest degree, just to survive. (Though it wasn't until recently that I could fully recognize it.) I was genuinely loving and caring toward others, but I didn't allow myself to be loved. I developed a deep level of shame and anger that put a guard around my heart, which even blocked out my Heavenly Father.

According to Proverbs 1:7 (NLT), "Fear of the Lord is the foundation of true knowledge." Here is where it went wrong for me. I feared God improperly, and because my lens was so damaged, I had no good reference point. I lived, for as long as I can remember, in a place of shame, never seeing God for who He really is. It was the goodness and love of God that I could never comprehend. Feelings of worthlessness distorted this "fear" into rebellion, leaving me with a misguided and false knowledge of the One who created me. We've all heard the saying, "Rules without relationship equals rebellion," and my friend, I am here to attest to that with blood, sweat, and tears. The most important factor to walking wisely in this life IS a healthy fear of the Lord, and you cannot expect to gain any Godly knowledge or wisdom if you don't first trust that He is good and loves you for who you are, not what you can produce. That healthy fear of the Lord is the substance that keeps you in His pocket of care and protection, open to His discipline, and submitted to His amazing will.

The sad fact remains, according to solid statistical evidence, as many as sixty to seventy percent of ALL men in the U.S. are addicted to pornography. Roughly fifty percent[3] of pastors and leaders are in the same place I was, ministering in brokenness and feeling as if they have nowhere to go. You may be like me and have lived a "good" Christian life, trying hard to please others, but you have secrets that nobody but God knows. You may have even convinced yourself, like I did, that you tricked God, or worse yet, that He doesn't really care about you, your pain, and your anger. You might be someone who has been struggling with pornography as I did, but won't share with anyone out of fear of what it might do to your life and those you love. I understand

---

3   Brenton Evans, "Till porn do us part," FireProofMyMarriage.com http://fireproofmymarriage.com/dload.php?file=_images/_needhelp/InternetSafety.pdf (accessed Mar. 19, 2015).

that some might be dealing with unforgiveness toward family members, pastors, friends, or even the church, and you have allowed your heart to become hardened to a point that you don't trust anyone. Or, maybe you have felt like you've been let down by God Himself, and you don't know how to open your heart to Him again, to love and be loved.

Teri and I are passionate about seeing people healed and set free, as Christ has healed and set us free. The church won't be a place of healing from this issue unless we start seeing those in the church healed. We can't expect others to come for help if we aren't willing to be honest and healed ourselves. I've had people tell me directly, "James, I have that dark closet that I won't allow anyone into—I will take it to my grave." Many others have opened up to me about their struggles and feel as if they have no place to go. Please don't live your life this way. I thought I was deserving of this kind of hopeless life, but God's deep love and commitment to you and me just won't allow that.

I know that the enemy of your soul doesn't want you to go any further in this book. He wants to keep all of our feet far from a place of freedom, both for ourselves and for others. He doesn't want any of us to experience the freedom and fulfillment that God has waiting for all who have faith in Him. Please know that Teri and I are praying for you as you take this journey. As you commit your life to health, we are on the same path heading in the same direction. As you continue forward, we encourage you to bring others with you and live vulnerably and authentically with them before God.

We humbly offer this prayer for you:

Dear Heavenly Father,

We pray for those who have chosen to pick up this book as a tool to help them navigate this journey of healing and restoration, and for anyone who has a heart to see others set free. We know that we all have to deal with brokenness to some degree, because we live in a fallen world, but Father, thank You for sending Your Son, Jesus, so we don't have to live with that baggage anymore or see any brother or sister labor under it either.

We pray in Jesus' name that You would remove every piece of baggage that has been placed on each person who chooses to walk out this journey. Give freedom to those who ask (Matthew 7:7). We pray that You would give each and every person on this journey the strength and perseverance to run the race that is set out before them, leaving every hindrance behind (Hebrews 12:1), and that they would remember to take courage each and every day knowing that You are with them wherever they go (Joshua 1:5). We pray for new hearts and lives today. We ask that You would breathe Your everlasting breath into the dry bones of hopelessness and despair, bringing Your new life (Ezekiel 37:1–14). Thank You, Jesus, for the love, forgiveness, and grace You have extended our way, even when we didn't deserve it (Ephesians 2:1–10). We speak Your power and blessing over all those who choose this day to join us on this journey of freedom.

In Jesus' name, amen!

May you experience the love of Christ, though it is too great to understand fully. Then you will be made complete with all the fullness of life and power that comes from God. Now all glory to God, who is able, through his mighty power at work within us, to accomplish infinitely more than we might ask or think. Glory to him in the church and in Christ Jesus through all generations forever and ever! Amen.
Ephesians 3:19–21 (NLT)

Chapter 2
FOUNDATIONS

*These words I speak to you are not incidental additions to
your life, homeowner improvements to your standard of living.
They are foundational words, words to build a life on. If you
work these words into your life, you are like a smart carpenter
who built his house on solid rock. Rain poured down, the river
flooded, a tornado hit—but nothing moved that house. It was
fixed to the rock. But if you just use my words in Bible studies
and don't work them into your life, you are like a stupid carpenter
who built his house on the sandy beach. When a storm rolled in
and the waves came up, it collapsed like a house of cards.*

Matthew 7:24–27 (The Message)

SUMMER 2014

I gaze out at the ocean at Zuma Beach in Malibu, California, and
I am in awe. My two younger daughters run back and forth in
the water, my eldest daughter laughs with her friends, and sitting
next to me is my steadfast wife. I am totally overwhelmed with
gratitude and thankfulness for our new and abundant life. When
I refer to abundant, I am making reference to the things money
can't buy: love, honesty, freedom, and vulnerability. As I reflect

back on this last year and a half, I am amazed that through the grace and power of God, our family has made it to this place, living vibrantly and in unity.

Many people who know me have asked, "How did you get from where you were to where you are now?" referring directly to the broken road we've traveled since starting my recovery and our family restoration. The day our lives changed forever, everything I had spent so much time and energy trying to conceal and cover was utterly exposed. This exposure brought me to my knees, and I remember vividly pleading with God for a second chance with Him and with my loving family. Many would ask, *How in the world did you get to that point in the first place?* The very raw fact is that I wasn't able to answer that question right away, and even more real is that it took me the better part of nine months of rigorous counseling to figure out what went wrong in my life and how to realign myself to the original purpose God had given to me before I was even born (Psalm 139). To some reading this testimonial, it might seem strange that I'm starting with a huge flashback to my childhood in order to unpack the baggage of my today, but as I found out in this healing process, the origin of my pain was key. Everything unattended to and not dealt with in my life progressively led to destructive behavioral patterns.

I was the youngest, and the scrawniest, in a family of six. I came into this world with all the life expectations of any precious child. I had a family who loved me and, in their way, wanted nothing but the best for me. Our family spent a great deal of time together. We were very active in life, church, and athletics. We worshipped together, were expected to participate in sports and community events, and were expected to succeed in all we laid our hands on. Our lives were busy; as the youngest child, I vividly remember trying desperately to keep up.

I also remember that each day came to a conclusion at the dinner table where we had some of the most dysfunctional experiences mingled with the most joyous. I'd sit, listen, and watch as things transpired, and learned to survive from the cues I observed. My siblings were ten, nine, and four years older than me, so it was inevitable that I watched a lot of life going on around me. I learned very young how to protect myself and cover my tracks so I wouldn't have to deal with the harsh punishments that came with any unpermitted behavior.

The Craft family was perfect on the outside. We were the family that went to church every Sunday morning and Sunday night, Wednesday night, and spent another night at Royal Rangers. We typically had some kind of small group taking place at our home. Each one of the Craft kids landed on the front of the sports page for athletics at one time or another and were viewed in our community as model citizens. The phrase "You can never judge a book by its cover" was a deep truth I struggled with most of my life. I love my family dearly to this day, and we still come together for special occasions to celebrate the goodness of God and His faithfulness displayed to each and every one of us, though this life has been anything but picture perfect.

In the first ten crucial years of my life I was shaped by the models I had in front of me, as are all children. If you could peek into my life at this young age, though seemingly perfect on the outside, you would see brokenness and abusive patterning was all around me. I've come to accept that life isn't fair and everyone is dealt a hand of cards, but how you play or respond to those cards will determine the outcome of your life. Until the recent healing, it had always made me very angry. I realize now that if you try to force or control the outcome in that place of anger, you will never find freedom or fulfillment in your purpose. This broken man eventually had to give up control, past and present, and allow the Creator of the universe, the God who knit me together in my mother's womb, to have control over the purpose He gave me, even if it started with a foundation of hurt and confusion.

At a very young age, I started questioning the calling of God on my life. I questioned where He was in my deepest pains, and as you will read, my life became a time bomb of Christian misinformation and total dysfunction. I had heard many times that "He will never leave us or forsake us" (Deuteronomy 31:6), but I had a hard time believing in its veracity. On many nights during my growing-up years, I cried myself to sleep. Where was God when I was in so much pain? Why didn't He comfort me? My mind and my image of God began to be tweaked and distorted. I could quote Deuteronomy 31:6, and eventually do a great illustrative teaching on it, but I didn't fully believe it in the bone and marrow of my existence. I was alone, unloved by God, and any comfort I'd find in life was up to me.

In those formative years, our family created pressure for me to be someone I wasn't. Though I don't think anyone intentionally did this, it was the system that was created. The origin of my parents' upbringing was passed on from the system they had lived under. I have a brother who is nine years older than me, and I always believed I had to be just like him to be successful. I had to play the same sports, achieve the same grades, have as many girlfriends, and the list goes on. I grew up believing that if you perform well, then you are loved well. But things don't always go that way. I never thought I was good enough in anything I did. Even though I could do better in different areas than my siblings, I always lived in their shadow—or so I believed.

In the early years of my life, if I felt I was failing or being rejected, I broke down and cried, hoping for an arm that would stretch out and draw me close to affirm and build up. Instead, crying became a point of shame in my life; my God-given sensitive heart was perceived as a weakness. In my family, joking and sarcasm were used as ways to escape the real issues of life. When I was between eight and ten years old, some of my siblings sang me a song that was supposed to be funny, but instead of building up, all it did was tear me down and continue to firmly establish deep shame and anger in my life. The song went like this: *"Jamie's a baby. He sucks his thumb. Nobody likes him because he cries all the time."* I hated that song, and no one, not even my parents, did anything about its damaging tune and the negative effects it created.

I honestly didn't know how to deal with all of this negativity, so I perfected the survival skill of compartmentalization. I laughed and then cried. I lashed out and then ran away. I desperately wanted to be held, but found comfort in isolation. Again, I must reiterate that all this knowledge was a total mystery of anger and confusion until my recent recovery and healing process. During this very vulnerable season of my early childhood, I was initially introduced to pornography by a fellow student, and though I will go into greater detail later regarding this issue in my life, it is very important to note that the hook was easily embedded into my unguarded and unprotected fragile life, with me not knowing the death and destruction it would later produce.

You might be asking where my parents were in this process. The answer is…right there. No one comprehended that this kind of living was wrong or damaging. It was all a big joke, or so it seemed. I was taught to laugh as the pain increased on the inside. I was supposed to laugh when rejection hit me between the eyes. I learned to laugh when I felt like a failure and no one was standing next to me. This coping mechanism was firmly established in my life as a survival tool. The real problem is, we're not created to develop coping mechanisms in our lives that ultimately bring isolation. We are not created to be in control, but we are called and encouraged by our Heavenly Father to give Him control so that we can live out our purpose in freedom and unhindered relationship with Him and others.

Many times in my life I got angry at one or both of my parents for not stepping in and stopping the madness in our house. I resented my parents for that until recently when I began to see where they stood in those times (which doesn't represent who they are today). I came to the understanding that my parents did the best they could with what they were given. They both experienced great trauma growing up, so they both had to learn how to cope with deep pain that their hearts harbored, much like the trauma I was surviving. When any kind of pain hit my dad, he isolated, wouldn't talk, and eventually blew up with extreme anger. This consisted of lashing out at my mom or us kids. I had few meaningful conversations with him in those early years. My mom's way of coping was through anger and pain medication that would take her out of her reality to a place where she wouldn't have to deal with the real issues before her.

So, I learned how to isolate and medicate the deep pain. I want to make sure you understand that I am not blaming my parents for the actions of my life; I am simply identifying the point of origin of the pain and the mechanisms I used to deal with that pain. I'm the first to understand the temptation to point a finger at those who have hurt you in the past and never deal with the real issues that are eating you alive. With great clarity and peace, I now understand that I must not blame, but reclaim what the enemy has stolen, and fight for true forgiveness—even if it takes months or years of intense counseling to achieve. I had to acknowledge that I carried a deep wound in my life, and because I didn't know how to access or identify that pain, or how to deal with it properly, it eventually drove me, and those I loved the most, off a steep cliff.

Dr. Ted told us, "Early on as a child, the trauma in the form of emotional and physical abuse shapes the structure and functioning of the brain in ways that negatively affect all stages of social, emotional, and intellectual development." This sobering truth represents how I dealt with the challenges I faced in life. Growing up, I saw conflict dealt with in our home through yelling and screaming, sarcasm, isolation, drug addiction, and, eventually, hair pulling or slapping. These patterns were deeply implanted in my brain as a way of dealing with tough issues. I didn't have healthy models to show how it could be done constructively. I didn't even know what isolation, abuse, and addiction were, let alone the evils of adopting such behavior.

You learn pretty fast that it is unsafe to open up to anyone in this kind of environment. Healthy communication and how God fit into it all were not part of our family dynamic, especially not with the youngest child who probably wasn't paying attention anyway, right? This confusing, two-faced type of lifestyle was all I knew. Being left on my own before the age of ten to figure it out and not knowing how to access the pain left me open to the only means I was being shown to cope, and that was medicating this worthless place in my life with isolation and whatever I could find on the outside that would take me away mentally.

Around the age of eleven, I was fed up with the teasing that took place because of my crying and sensitivity. One of the ways I coped with my pain was by making a vow never to cry or lose to anyone again. This not only shut me down emotionally, but it also started me on a path of hardness that drove any empathy that was left in my heart far from me and gave sarcasm free rein.

I started to see everything and everyone as opponents, not really knowing what it was to open my heart to healthy relationships. I started to see my life as one big competition to prove my worth and value.

Athletics was a large part of my life all the way through college, and victory meant approval and love. Failure, on the other hand, meant shame and defeat. For a young man growing up, not having a model to lead me through these darkest moments in my life, caused me to start to lose my way, stumbling and falling with no positive benchmark I could trust. I desperately wanted and needed a guide to show me how to become the young man I was created to be. When no one stepped up to the plate, not even my father, the feeling of disappointment and the sense of rejection in my life led me deeper into unforgiveness, anger, and resentment. I allowed this to become my identity, which masked the brokenness and insecurity that I put so much energy into covering up. The vow I made as a boy formed and shaped who I became in my twenties and beyond.

Throughout my teen years, the anger in my heart increased. My mom was battling addiction to pain medication the best she could and wasn't mentally or even physically present for most of those years. The older I got, I saw my dad become more distant and isolated. My brother and sisters moved out of the house, and I avoided coming home whenever possible. I stayed late at school for sports, which gave me an excuse to not go home at regular times and provided me extra fuel for my need to win at everything I signed my name to. As I look back at this time in my life, I see clearly that it was a defining stage where I allowed compartmentalization to take root. When I was at home, I could easily shut down and distance myself from the pain. And when I was on the field, or in church or school leadership, I could engage with confidence and competence. If I was with friends, I acted as if everything was perfect and gave the impression that I was living the best life anyone could ask for.

At fifteen I met the love of my life, Teri. We were in a pre–algebra class together, and then eventually youth group, where we first began a friendship. We started dating the following year, and she became the closest friend I ever had. We were always together with our group of friends and developed a relationship that revolved around church, her family, and school. Teri would come over to my house on occasion, but we spent most of our time at her house. I felt ashamed and embarrassed at what she might see at my home. In this season of my life, I started to control my environment without even knowing what I was doing. When it was safe, then we'd be at my house. When it wasn't, I would make sure we stayed far away.

This control started to dictate every area of my life, forcing me to live with fear of rejection and failure everywhere I went. I kept everyone at a distance, not allowing myself to be vulnerable. As I look back, I can see that I had many friends, but never any true friends who knew me inside and out. Teri and I grew very close while we were dating, but early in our relationship, there were doors I wouldn't allow her to open. We remained pure in our physical relationship and were married at the age of twenty, and for twenty–one years I regret to say I kept some of those awful compartments from her.

Through the rest of my teenage years and into my twenties, I continued the facade, making sure that my image was one of strength, security, and success. But the wounds of rejection and shame continued to grow from the inside out. I grew in favor with those around me, but I longed for something more. My addiction to porn intensified as I tried to outpace the increasing pain level. The more the addiction and pain grew, so did the lie I used to cover it up. I became a master of the double life, an echo of my childhood patterning. I compartmentalized every aspect of my life to maintain order in the chaos.

No success, person, or even my wounded perception of God could fill the void or take away the pain. I didn't know how to communicate what was wrong. How could I? I didn't understand it myself. The vow I made in my pre–teen years to succeed at all costs was spinning my life out of control. In my mind, I'd tell myself, *if you keep going, the pain will go away*. So, this nightmare went on into my twenties and thirties, until my identity was solely found in the job I was performing. I didn't know who I was or what I was called to do. People applauded me for growing a youth group, introducing a national vision, or my work as a senior pastor; but in all of that I was that little boy running scared and ready for a fight. This life drove me into a pit of shame, worthlessness, and hopelessness.

You might be wondering why I didn't turn to God, but I saw God as the judge who sat on His thrown with His finger pointing at me, telling me I was a failure. I can't express in words the exuberant joy and peace that came the day when I was able to forgive my earthly father. Subsequently, something broke in my heart toward my Abba Father. I no longer see God as angry with me, but now I see Him with arms open wide, longing for me to climb into His lap and experience His pure love for me.

I pause to interject that those years of ministry were a beautiful example of God's sovereign love given through me as an instrument of life to others. Though I realize now that so much of my inner focus was misguided and my personal choices were ultimately very hurtful, I give God all the glory for any and all good that came to others through my existence.

I've come to realize that the sensitive heart the Lord gave me was not a weakness. I ministered for years in brokenness, not understanding that the sensitive heart He gave me was to be used to bind me together with Christ and to allow me to love authentically and vulnerably those in my reach. The thing He gave me as a strength, I had seen as a weakness. I used everything at my disposal to cover it up and pretend it wasn't there.

Our foundations are meant to stand the test of time, strong and uncompromised. Mine may have given me strength for the short run, but not for the long haul. They isolated me. Crippled me. Lied to me. The freedom and security I could have found in my Heavenly Father, I searched for in other things. I don't share this to point the finger of blame at those who raised me, or even wronged me; I'm not trying to dodge my responsibility in my subsequent actions either, but to help you understand. When the foundations of a young person's existence are fractured and never mended, they eventually collapse under the pressure of life.

Those hurts and pains early in my life developed deep anger and destructive patterns in my heart and mind that drove away every person who tried to come close to me. Because I didn't deal with that anger I had toward my father and family until later in life, I was bound and hardened in my heart from the true love of my Heavenly Father. No matter what your foundation may look like, I encourage you from one who knows the rocky road of life, there is hope and healing.

Hear my heart, friend. I need for you to know God is into *process*. He hasn't given up on any of us, no matter how far we have strayed. His loving hand started working on my heart the moment I turned a fraction of an inch from His will, though I wouldn't see the fulfillment of that redemptive plan until I was forty-one years old. Walk out your journey, no matter how difficult, in daily honesty and transparency before God and with those to whom you are accountable. What God is doing in you today is a part of a master plan He has for your life to bring you to ultimate freedom. Don't give up or be discouraged with where you are today. If you…

Trust in the Lord with all of your heart, and lean not on your own understand, in all your ways acknowledge Him, and He will make your path straight.
Proverbs 3:5–6

Chapter 3
IN PURSUIT

Yes, I have loved you with an everlasting love;
therefore with lovingkindness I have drawn you.

Jeremiah 31:3 (NKJV)

Words sometimes can't bring a concrete expression to the stifling emotional state people find themselves in when they've shut their heart off in places for decades. It's a cold place. It's lonely, and it feels as close to hopelessness as you can get. What's worse is that some, like me, don't even realize it has happened until we're miles down the road. It begins to feel more like home to be walled up than to live in freedom. As I've been navigating this new journey, I am amazed and heartbroken at the staggering number of men who live exactly as I did.

You read in the last chapter the circumstances that contributed to my life of addiction and brokenness. I didn't have to stay there, and neither do any of you who find yourselves in deep places of woundedness. There is an out, and it begins and ends with the Lord, Adonai. Since I was so shut off and guarded, I forgot what it felt like to be touched by the pursuant and unconditional love of the Father. I found myself many times in the recovery process crying out to God, and sometimes getting angry with Him saying, "Where were you in my pain?" much like what I asked as a child. But as I began to allow Him to chip away at the walls that had been forged around my heart and life, I began to see His love story woven throughout my life.

I vividly remember the Lord reminding me of His undying love one day in my morning prayer and devotion time. I had turned to Luke 15, a passage of scripture the men in my Pure Desire group and I had talked about the day before. My posture that early morning was simply, *Lord, show me You in relation to the broken me*, and I began to read the parable of the lost son. My eyes welled up with tears as the words rose off the page like a cinematic masterpiece. I could hardly contain myself when I came to **this**:

And while he was still a long way off, his father saw him
coming. Filled with love and compassion,
he ran to his son, embraced him, and kissed him.
His son said to him, "Father, I have sinned against both heaven
and you, and I am no longer worthy of being called your son."

But his father said to the servants, "Quick!
Bring the finest robe in the house and put it on him.
Get a ring for his finger and sandals for his feet. And kill the
calf we have been fattening. We must celebrate with a feast,
for this son of mine was dead and has now returned to life.
He was lost, but now he is found." So the party began.
Luke 15:20–24

I sat for some time taking in this genuine moment with the Lord. "I've done the same for you," the soft, kind voice said to my heart. At my kitchen table, I was coming to the revelation of the unconditional love my Father has for me through His Word. My friend, the Lord of Life loves us all so much that He will run to us, even when we are far off in the distance, embrace us, and lead us home. Take a moment and let that sink in. I love this! Don't read this as just a story. Don't read this as a textbook. Read it as *your* story. God sees you in the distance: dirty, disheveled, broken and wholly undone. He runs to *you*. He drops all He is doing and He runs to *you*. He throws His arms around your stinky carcass and He cries tears of joy because *you* are home!

"This is Me in relation to you," the Lord declared to my broken soul. I could have done cartwheels down the street when that truth grabbed my heart! Another piece of the wall fell from my heart that day.

During any recovery process it is essential to identify the origins of pain and woundedness that drive behavior. It is also a very healing exercise to remember the God–moments in your life story. Dr. Ted was good at asking the right questions at the right time to draw out the hidden treasures that had been lost or forgotten. "God was there in your pain, James. You need to rediscover what He was doing and saying in those prophetic moments."

This may sound like an easy assignment, but trust me, it's a hard one when you're emotionally, physically, and spiritually drained. I asked the Lord to bring me hope by showing me His faithfulness. I heard His still, small voice remind me, "I was there, James, even when you didn't know it." Just then a memory came clearly to mind.

I served as associate pastor at a church in Danville, California, from 2000 to 2007, while simultaneously serving as the National

Youth Director for the Foursquare denomination. I had two full–time jobs, ran a youth ministry with over 400 kids, traveled around the nation speaking at conferences and churches, all the while directing a global event that brought 7,000 young people from around the world together in Anaheim, California. In all of the busyness of ministry and family, I served under one of the best pastors I've ever known, Pastor Ron Pinkston. Ron and I worked really well together, but we were complete opposites. He was mild–mannered, and I was the crazy one ready to take on the world at all costs. Ron was calculating, and I was impulsive. We were, however, very similar in our passion for those who were broken and lost—ironic, I know.

I focused more on those who were broken in the world around me and he focused on the brokenness that had taken place in me. I didn't really like this kind of attention in my life at the time; I knew if I allowed him too close, he might see that I was really worthless and shameful. Ron pushed on the boundaries and walls I had built around my heart. I could see he cared for me and my family and not just what we accomplished.

I remember, like it was yesterday, a time I shared with Ron that touched my life deeply, and I perceive now that it was a catalyst that began unraveling the bound places in my heart, a process that ultimately took over thirteen years to complete. We had been in Danville about four months. I came onto the scene as a spitfire youth pastor ready to break down the gates of hell. The world was our harvest and no one was going to stop us from reaping it. As I started to get my feet planted on the ground, I began to run into other staff members who didn't seem to move at my speed and didn't seem to have the same passion I had for the lost. As I mentioned before, I've come to realize that God gifted me with a sensitive heart for those who are hurting and lost. Reaching out to them is what I was meant to do. But in my dysfunction, my drive and application had become unhealthy. As I introduced new ideas to become more outward–focused to reach those in need, I bumped up against staff who didn't share the same focus or understand my zeal. In my mind, I thought this was the ultimate call for the church…reach the lost at all costs. After all, this was the imprint the Lord had given me from birth. What I didn't realize was that because of my hurt and brokenness, this God–given passion took on an unhealthy focus, so much so that I began to hurt others with the very gift my Father in Heaven had given me to touch the world with His love and gentleness.

One day, I came to a breaking point with one of the staff members. I couldn't handle it any longer. I started questioning why in the world we moved to Danville in the first place. Was I being punished for some reason? After having a blowup with this staff member (who later became a dear brother and friend to me), I marched myself right up to Pastor Ron's office to share with him how our church was doing it all wrong. I was angry, and knew it showed all over my face. Though I can't confirm it, there may have been smoke coming from my ears. I entered the room where Pastor Ron's assistant was working and announced that I needed to talk with Pastor right now. She could tell that I wasn't messing around and called him right away, asking if he was available to meet with me. He didn't hesitate, and asked me to come right in.

I remember sitting in front of his large, executive desk, while he finished what he was working on. He started the conversation by saying, "How's it going, James?" I thought in my mind, *Are you serious for asking me that?* So, I let him have it. I went on for fifteen minutes, letting him know all the things that we were doing wrong as a church, how dysfunctional our staff was, and questioning if we were having any impact in our community. Our church was about 1,500 people at that time and served a very affluent region filled with executives, entrepreneurs, and self-starters. The truth was that our church was having great impact on our region, state, and nation, but all I could see was life and ministry through my tainted lenses.

After giving my patient pastor the leadership lecture of the decade, a thought flashed across my mind, *What did I just do? He is going to fire me right on the spot.* I was completely out of control and reckless. The anger that came from me that day was destructive and harmful, not only to me, but also to everyone around me. After I finished my little temper tantrum, I braced myself for the backlash I knew was due me, all while thinking, *Why do I do what I don't want to do?*

Something started to shift for me as I observed Pastor Ron's demeanor and his non-verbal cues, which were very calm and peaceful. He saw right through my lecture, looked straight into my heart, and saw a wounded man. He understood that in this state of brokenness, anger and rage came flowing out of me, but that wasn't the "me" I was called to be. Instead of pointing his finger in my direction, correcting and defending everything the church had done and was doing, he got up from his chair, and walk around to where I was sitting.

For a moment I thought, *Maybe I was wrong…maybe I'm dead. Maybe here in Danville they do things a little differently. Maybe violence was the answer and I needed to get my backside kicked and sent back to work.* But what happened next was a game-changer for me. He grabbed the other chair that was sitting next to me, sat down, and turned it my way. You have to understand, at this point, my heart rate was sky high; adrenaline was flowing through my veins at top speed and I could feel myself getting defensive and ready to self–preserve. Pastor Ron, however, showed me something different from anything I had ever experienced in my life. He showed me love, peace, and compassion in my time of need. There was no shame–based language used that day, no demeaning, no yelling or screaming. No negative retribution to be handed out, just love and compassion. I experienced a father reaching out to a son and extending a hand of love with no expectation in return. This was the first time in my thirty–something years of life to have this type of encounter.

When Pastor Ron sat down next to me, he kindly asked me to turn my chair to face him. He looked at me with his gentle eyes and asked if he could wash my feet. My mind was ablaze with confusion as I thought to myself, *Are you crazy? First of all, I don't want anyone touching my feet, and second, this is not the time for something like this!* But that is not what came out of my mouth, I blurted out a fumbling, "Yes." It took my breath away to see him get on his knees, take his hands and place them on my shoes, and start to pray. At first, I didn't understand. I didn't get it. The truth was, leaders in my life didn't do this. Adults had never done this in a time of conflict, why was he?

He started to pray that all the things that had stuck to me on my journey of life that weren't supposed to be there would be washed away. He prayed that the hurt, pain, rejection, and disappointment would be unhinged by the love of Christ. I started to cry. This wasn't any ordinary cry. I started to cry like I hadn't cried for the last decade, and the dam finally broke loose. That is exactly what was happening. When Pastor Ron prayed for those specific areas of my life, he hit a wound that I vowed at a very young age I would never allow anyone to touch again. On that day, the Lord reminded me that He loved me too much to leave me the way I was. Although it took much longer and involved much more pain and hurt than I or anyone affected could have imagined, the work my loving Father started that day has finally come to fruition in my life, and it came by way of a life–saving touch woven deep into the redemptive plan of my Savior.

Why did the Lord bring this memory back to me in the dark–valley moment of my recovery process? I believe He wanted to remind me that He was right there with me presently and that He had been there along the way. This reminder was not delivered through condemnation like an "I told you so," statement or "Duh, it took you long enough to finally get it, buddy." Rather, it was a sweeter–than–honey reminder helping me hear the rhythm of my Father's heart. He was reiterating the words of Jeremiah 31:3 (NKJV) "Yes, I have loved you with an everlasting love; therefore with loving–kindness I have drawn you." The Good Shepherd was guiding me, knowing that so much was at stake in my life, marriage, and the legacy of our precious girls. If I was unable to remember and connect my heart with my Creator in this new place, I would be no good for anyone. That hard heart Jesus had been working on for years was now exposed on the surgery table. I needed to allow the process, uncomfortable as it was, to take place. In all the hardening in my life and the choices that came from that place, I had forgotten what the touch of Jesus felt like.

I recall sitting at our dining table doing my daily devotion and Pure Desire workbook assignment, feeling as if I was pushing back an onslaught of hell meant to derail me and our family from finding freedom and restoration. I cried out to the Lord, "Help me, Jesus!" My loving Savior responded gently with, "I am willing," and I felt prompted to read Mark 1:40–42 (NKJV).

Now a leper came to Him, imploring Him,
kneeling down to Him and saying to Him, "If You are willing,
You can make me clean." Then Jesus, moved with compassion,
stretched out His hand and touched him, and said to him,
"I am willing; be cleansed." As soon as He had spoken,
immediately the leprosy left him, and he was cleansed.

The words were three–dimensional to me; I could see the whole scenario taking place, and I could see myself in the very footprints of that leper. How hopeless at times he must have felt. How shamefully others treated him in his infirmity. Hope came on the scene when Jesus entered this man's city. The leper knelt down and worshiped Him. "If you are willing, You can make me clean," he uttered with all the faith he could muster (Mark 1:40 NKJV). The amazing thing is that the passage goes on to state, "then Jesus, moved with compassion, stretched out His hand and touched him, and said, 'I am willing, be cleansed.'" Tears streamed down my face, as once again I was touched by my Savior's love that was healing my scars and dismantling my walls. The Lord was whispering to the innermost parts of my soul, "I love you, James." For the first time in my life I was starting to get it…really get it.

I began to see my past life in terms of my dysfunction and how that was related to my disconnect with Him. I had been running so hard and fast TOWARD Jesus, trying to perform for His approval, that I forgot to put my hand out and touch Him. I was so afraid of letting Him down that I convinced myself He wasn't willing to heal me, the outcast. Thanks to the story of the leper and the faithful touch Jesus extended to me, I can now say to you, friend, He is willing. Don't be afraid to reach out and touch Him. Better yet, let Him touch you. In that touch lives freedom, and oh, what a freedom it is!

Dear Heavenly Father,

As I think back through the pain and challenges of my life, I now see that You stood by my side in my early years of confusion and even in the madness I created. I see Your gentle eyes looking on me with compassion as I walked, many times to the beat of my own drum. You never gave up on me, and You were cheering me on with words of affirmation, not condemnation. You always extended forgiveness to me rather than judgment; gentleness instead of anger. While I saw You through my lens of pain and shame, Your loving view of me never changed. In my deepest pain and brokenness, You were there for me with arms open wide to draw me close. It was in that time and place that I experienced the true love that You have always had for me.

Please forgive me for pushing You away. Cleanse me from the distorted memory I had of You for so many years. I repent for blemishing Your beautiful Bride, and not caring for her as You have cared for me. Forgive me for every misguided and willful decision I made in rebellion against You, and wash my loved ones clean of any residue associated with my sinful choices.

I put You in a box along with my hurt and pain, never allowing myself to be fully one with You…until now. Thank You for removing the dirty lens on my life so I can see Your heart and love for me, and for those You have entrusted to my care. Never again do I want to be away from You, separated from You in that dark and lonely place. I love You always and with every breath. I commit to walking hand in hand with You until the day I am fully in Your presence. Give me strength to get back up when I fall and grace to walk again.

James

Chapter 4
DON'T GO ALONE

There are no hurdles in this life we can't overcome together with our Father as our protector and guide. The key is remembering that life is not a sprint; it's a marathon.

Track and field has been a major part of my life, from childhood to when I was awarded a Division 1 college scholarship at Fresno State University in sprinting. I think I was born running fast. It's about all I remember doing as a kid. But running long distance, well, that's another story all together. I've run thousands of races in my life, but the hardest race I ever ran came on March 9, 2014.

I had been helping raise funds for the rescue mission my brother founded and operated, and had this crazy idea, "Why don't we run the Los Angeles Marathon to help raise money and bring awareness to the cause of helping the homeless in LA?" Some of you might not think that's such a crazy idea; however, it was only two weeks until the running of the 26.2 mile race. I called my brother to pitch the idea, and all I heard on the other side of the line was silence. I went on to say, "I know if we do this together, stick with each other the entire race, we can finish it." There was another long pause, and then I heard, "Okay. I'm in!"

So, after some preparation, minimal conditioning, and planning, we found ourselves at Dodger Stadium early that March morning with 25,000 other runners from across the globe. It was one of the most amazing sights I'd ever witnessed. Imagine 25,000 people alive with excitement and anticipation for the long road ahead. When the race started, we were swept up in the exuberant momentum of the festivities, which took us through the first eight miles. After that, we had to start thinking about our own pace and plan in order to finish the race and receive the donations that had been pledged for the rescue mission. Throughout the race, we took turns encouraging each other and reminding the other to drink water, eat our energy gels, and stay on pace.

It's hard to explain the camaraderie we shared with everyone running that day. It was literally as if we were all on the same team, there to help each other get across the finish line. When someone fell, people would run over and help him or her up. When we started to slow down and look as if we were going to stop, a fellow runner would call out in passing, "You can do it! Don't give up!" Even the crowds were completely electric. We passed marching bands, cheerleaders, and a couple of guys dressed like Elvis Presley. The miles melted away as we ran, or walked at times in our case, past the most iconic landmarks in Los Angeles: the Hollywood Walk of Fame, Chinatown, Rodeo Drive, and the Hollywood Sign, to name a few.

When we hit mile twenty, it was an all–out battle to even take another step. We realized we had to depend on each other if we were going to make it to the end. I remember coming down the street in Santa Monica and seeing the Pacific Ocean come into view. All the pain and exhaustion of the past twenty–five miles took a back seat, and we focused on finishing the race. Pressing on together, we crossed that finish line side by side, accomplishing the goal of running the LA Marathon and raising $25,000 for the rescue mission. Honestly, there was no way for either of us to have completed the race without the support of the other. Before we even began, we made the pledge that we would stay together and finish together or die trying!

> *It's better to have a partner than go it alone.*
> *Share the work, share the wealth. And if one falls down,*
> *the other helps, but if there's no one to help, tough!*
> Ecclesiastes 4:9–10 (The Message)

I have come to a new understanding through my recovery process: I am not called to live alone. You might be thinking, "Duh, doesn't everyone know that?" Well, I guess I never read the memo, because I lived in what I'd call "populated isolation" for most of my life in an attempt to protect the wounded side of James Craft. I use the term "populated isolation" because I was rarely alone, but dwelling deep inside me was a vault locked tight and soldered shut. The problem with this kind of living is that every time I'd relapse or the pain would well up in me due to outside triggers, the dark side of James would come out and I'd push away everyone in my life. This mode of living allowed people in, up to an arm's length, but if anything became uncomfortable I was able to step away before they could hurt me.

I know I'm not alone. There are others who live their lives this way. Like me, they have parts of their heart they won't open to any person, let alone God. This kind of thinking and living creates a damaging barrier between a person's heart and the ultimate expression of love and acceptance given first and foremost by their Creator. I've learned the hard way that in order to experience this love and acceptance from the Lord, I have to be postured in such a way as to accept it. I have to surrender to it. It's there for the receiving.

Accepting that my tender heart was a gift from God helped me recognize that it was the primary target of the enemy's destructive war against my life. It is with this tender-hearted fingerprint of my Heavenly Father that I could minister to others and easily accept people in whatever state they were in. I genuinely cried for the lost and broken, and often was the one who could see the hidden potential in the rebellious or wandering soul. I could be on the mission field or communicating to a person about Jesus in that tenderness, but a shift would happen in my thinking anytime someone would get too close or rub up against the pain receptors of failure or rejection. When that happened, I would revert to my isolated and self-preserving ways. I had no tender heart toward myself, only shame and the fear of punishment.

The key here is that I lived in my gifting to a certain point, but because I couldn't get past my hurt long enough to be vulnerable in my relationship with my Heavenly Father, I couldn't accept me. So, I would do as the child in me did: take a piece of that tender heart, shove it in the vault, and lock it up tight. What was it I really longed for, but couldn't annunciate? I desperately wanted to be known, but I didn't know how to "be" —to be okay with the James God created me to be, to be vulnerable with my Father in Heaven, to be in His presence and not feel shame or worthlessness, just to be loved. I didn't know how to surrender.

The hardcore healing from my life of isolation started when I was required to attend a Pure Desire men's group. This is a small group of men committed to walking through the *Seven Pillars of Freedom* by Dr. Ted Roberts. I remember the first time I went to the group while we were still living in Hawaii. I showed up at the church, nervous, sweating profusely, and feeling utterly confused and hopeless. People looked at me because they recognized who I was, but the Hawaiian people responded like they always did, with great love and grace. When I first sat down I told myself, "Today is a new beginning, James. Today you are going to be honest about where you have been and where you are right now." I made a commitment that day to be transparent and lay it all on the table. I realized that enough is enough. I had handed over far too much of my life and damaged too many others not to crush the "populated isolation" monster once and for all.

In my hand I clutched the little Ebenezer stone my wife had brought back from our stay at the North Shore cottage that she describes in her writing. She had placed this profound reminder in my hand right before I left our townhome that morning to journey half-way across the island to where the meeting was held. I remember telling my story in a shaking voice, thinking it was going to shock the other guys in the room. It didn't. They each had their own story of pain, confusion, and isolation, and now we all sat in a room together on common ground, laying open our hearts to one another without judgment or condemnation. Where once I would have thought this would identify a man as weak, I now saw only broken men who were strong and courageous. I was only able to meet with those men in Hawaii for one month, but I bonded with them more than I had with any other men up to that point.

We eventually moved back to Southern California, and Dr. Ted asked that I join an online Pure Desire group with four other men located in Florida, Canada, and Oregon. We joined together every Monday evening for two hours to process, confess, encourage, challenge, and pray for each other. We became the unshakable brotherhood I always longed for, but never had. I finally learned what it was like to have a brother in Christ stand with me no matter what took place. Whether circumstances were good or bad, our commitment to one another was unwavering.

I've had many acquaintances in life, but very few true friends. I mean the kind that are spoken of in Proverbs 17:17, "A friend loves at all times, and a brother is born for a time of adversity." My previous friends typically consisted of those individuals who were connected with me for what I did, not who I was; I confess that was mostly of my making.

My wife and I were amazed by how alone we felt after the news hit the airwaves about my choices and the battle we faced as a family. At first, we were deeply hurt that so many of the people in our former life just vanished, but we decided to do the right thing and ask God what He was doing in the midst of it. He revealed that it was only through healing that we would understand more fully and walk more grace–filled toward our fellow man. Dr. Ted also opened our hearts to the fact that people will most often respond out of their lens of hurt and perception based on their own life circumstances and whether or not they themselves have been courageous enough to be healed. With the help of my men's group, I began to see clearly that I had kept most of my relationships shallow because my pain was deep, and that many of my former acquaintances were struggling with the same tendency. This is why my Pure Desire Group felt unnatural at first. It felt like I was given new skin to live in, which was as uncomfortable as trying to put on stiff, unwashed jeans for the first time.

While Teri, the girls, and I were battling to re–establish the foundation of our lives, I had a couple of great friends who drew closer to me and allowed me to fumble through my recovery without judgment and shame. Our friends Antonio and Cheryl were a Godsend to our family. They had attended the church Teri and I once pastored. I had married and even baptized them, but now they came to us as ministers of the tangible love of Jesus. They had nothing to gain from us; in fact, it was probably the juicy talk of many for a season that they would open their home to our family. But they chose to offer what we needed the most, and that was unconditional love. It was obvious that their hearts were broken from our misguided past choices, but there were no stones thrown our way. There were only open arms to help us back on our feet, pointed in the right direction.

Our pastors and friends, Gary and Tammy, also took a great deal of time to care for our family in such a way that helped us open our hearts to a deeper level of this new, healthy living to which we were being introduced. I recall one specific occasion when Pastor Gary asked the congregation to get up from their seats and pray throughout the sanctuary. We were still in our early stages of new life, so the shame and hurt was still pretty raw in us. Therefore, we made a beeline for the back corner and huddled together like a group of outcasts. The next thing we knew, Pastor Gary was coming right for us and we could tell he was on a mission. He grabbed me tight then placed his hands around my face and said, "James, don't you forget that you are still in God's plan A." Then he gently told our daughter Rachel, "God is pleased with your heart." We circled around, all crying at this point, and prayed. I will forever be changed by that encounter of love and Christ–centered authority. Gary was a willing vessel used by the living God to encourage us that He is sovereign and that His plan is perfect, even when we are not.

Since I was no longer in church ministry, I had to find a job that would provide for my family. In our pursuit to be in the Lord's will regarding everything we laid our hands to, we prayed fervently to be in a place that would allow flexibility to continue our healing process and be very present in our girls' lives. God faithfully aligned me with my dear friend Dave. He approached me about starting a company that would benefit and serve churches and nonprofit organizations. Teri and I agreed that it was the Lord, so with great excitement, and a whole lot of faith, we prepared for the new journey ahead. As I look back to that fragile time in our lives, I can see God's hand all over us as a family. Though our circumstances weren't easy, and it took everything in us to stay the course when things got hard, we are amazed by and grateful for the miracles Jesus performed on our behalf. We found that the best remedy in times of need is to give generously. The more we opened our hearts to this posturing, the more the Lord did in our lives.

When I refer to "more," I am making reference first and foremost to the healing and restoration that was going on in our personal lives and relationships. It's apparent that God partnered us with a man who would not only challenge us in our entrepreneurial skills and offer much needed provision, but would also stretch us as we learned the fundamentals of business and financial planning. It was in this training season of my life that my dear friend and partner challenged me in my understanding of my Father God's character. I'd always said that I knew Jesus, but I had a hard time connecting with the Father. Dave kindly processed with me about God the Father and how much He loved His children.

Not only did we learn how to start a business from scratch, but I also discovered the heart of God the Father and His love for me. At the same time, I was reading legal contracts, learning the intricacies of a start–up company, creating business plans, and making phone calls. God was orchestrating a masterpiece that included outside, healthy relationships to drive home the concepts I was learning through the intense, internal re–patterning.

The title of this chapter is *Don't Go Alone*. I've relearned the proper rhythm of life in healthy relationships. I can't go any further without speaking of the new relationship I share with my wife, Teri. Back in the late 1980s when we were in high school, we started our relationship as best friends. We did just about everything together: church youth group, recreation, school, and family events. As our relationship grew stronger during high school and into our college years, we realized God had brought us together for life. Barring God, Teri is the most important person in my life. The heartbreaking truth is that in the past I didn't treat her the way Christ would have had me demonstrate His love, the kind that is described in Ephesians 5:25–28 (The Message), to her:

Husbands, go all out in your love for your wives, exactly as Christ did for the church—a love marked by giving, not getting. Christ's love makes the church whole. His words evoke her beauty. Everything he does and says is designed to bring the best out of her, dressing her in dazzling white silk, radiant with holiness. And that is how husbands ought to love their wives.

The health and closeness that we now share has created an environment of transparency, openness, and vulnerability that we never had before. We are complete when we are one, and it is this oneness that God intended for us when we first said, "I will." Teri and I have talked about what we will look like and be doing when we get old, and there is one reason we can have this kind of conversation—we fought hard. She didn't give up on me when she had every right to, and we are fully committed to each other to the very end. In the truest sense, it was when I laid my wounds and sin at the cross with repentance, forgave those in my past, and accepted the fervent love of the Father, that my heart became aware of the transparent love I needed to share with my wife, my ultimate helpmate and co–armor–bearer.

When the walls of isolation were annihilated, a powerful love story emerged, a story shared both by my Creator and my wife. The longing in my heart that had been such a point of confusion and hopelessness was satisfied in an instant by an eternal love that then spilled over to all the relationships I had been given here on earth, but started first with her. I consider it an honor to daily lay my life down, offer my purest love, subdue my personal desires, and communicate my most intimate thoughts and motivations to my forever love, my wife, Teri.

It has been through this process of healing, restoration, and surrender that I have discovered that healthy relationships are a necessity, rather than a threat. It is God's Plan A for all of us to be in a right relationship with Him and those He has entrusted to us. This wonderful knowledge helped bring healing to my heart where I had only seen hurt. As the pain was exposed and dug up through this recovery process, it was our healthy relationships that provided the very best environment for us to grow in the Lord. No longer do I have to earn my friendships through performance–based endeavors, or stress that maybe they really don't care about me. I am able to experience them by just being me, the whole and transparent me. There's no confusion regarding the fact that we have a journey ahead of us, but when we work and live vulnerably together, we can finish the race the way God intended, similarly to the way my brother Ken and I enjoyed running that marathon race because we were together.

Teri and I recognize that we will always have hurdles and struggles; that's what life on earth looks like. But there are no hurdles in this life we can't overcome together with our Father as our protector and guide. The key is remembering that life is not a sprint; it's a marathon.

James,

I am writing to say hello! I wonder if you remember the first time we met. You were a youth pastor, and Tammy & I were being trained to plant a church. We were at a conference and your youth band led worship one evening. When I met you, I was interested in getting to know you more fully. After several years of being acquaintances, I found myself still waiting to meet the real James Craft. As I have walked with you as a friend and a pastor through your recovery and restoration, I understand now the life of isolation you lived even though you had a very public role as a pastor. Hearing your honesty regarding this creates an empathetic response in me of how difficult your life was. This past year has been such a contrast to the former years of your existence. I have finally met the "real you." I have watched you learn to process life in a new and healthy way. I enjoy observing you be responsive and responsible to Teri as her husband. I have watched you transition from being Rachel's coach to being her dad that is coaching her heavenward. I see the gentle nudges you give Elise as you and Teri develop the fire of purpose that is in this young leader. If you could see the expression on your face when you talk to Grace, your youngest, I believe you would smile the way many of us do as we witness this doting father who could have lost his beautiful relationship with her, but now enjoys her lovingly gaze fixed right back at you. I no longer see fear in your eyes when you look at your family. There is a deep connection in the Craft family. What a difference a year can make when you walk honestly and vulnerably through the process of restoration.

As I think about how well your family is doing, I am also reminded of the friendships you have started in our church. James, you are a courageous man. You have allowed what the enemy meant for evil to be used for good. You have owned your mistakes, confessed your sins, learned a new way to process life, and you have stuck with the process until you developed into a new man. You have become an example to others who may be living a life of addiction or compartmentalization, who may be wondering if it is worth it to come out of hiding and walk away from the isolation. The answer is, "Yes!" I have seen your family be challenged and succeed in reprogramming their brains and reforming their relationships. I wish others could see your family interact, live in honesty, process challenges, pray together, and play together. You are a testimony that coming out of the shadows is worth it! It is a joy to be around you. I started this letter by saying "hello" because you are a new man in Christ. You no longer hide behind laughter and busy talk, but you present yourself as a person open to connection. It took years for you to leave isolation and become a person who is interdependent with others. I am so glad you did, you are a man that is worth knowing! I'm glad you finally believe it!!

With respect,
Pastor Gary

FINISHING STRONG: MY OBSERVATIONS OF SMALL GROUP DISCIPLESHIP

BY TYLER J. CHINCHEN
Marriage & Family Therapist
Certified Sex Addiction Therapist

In various roles and responsibilities since 1995, I've had the privilege to work with a multitude of people and family systems. From incarcerated youth, to men who struggle with sex addiction, to couples in marital crisis and families fighting for their very survival, all have sought help, or were forced to seek help, to move from destructive habits and behaviors into a healthy and honest relationship with others. Most sought positive change. Some were successful, others were not.

What characteristics helped influence a positive outcome for each? For many, the primary agent of change was the *individual's willingness to do the hard work and to finish strong*. Change is not easy. Change requires commitment to a new process. Change requires releasing control and trusting others. Change is difficult, often intimidating, and sometimes paralyzing. Change requires the resilience and fortitude to finish strong.

In the summer of 2013, I met James Craft. James was essentially thrust into change. One component of the change process for James was integration into a small group with other men who also sought change and restoration. This was new for James. No other guy, let alone a group of guys, had ever known all of James' story: the areas of pain, self–doubt, and insecurity. He had covered it well behind a facade called performance.

During the many weeks and months of meeting regularly with the group, James experienced change. He rarely missed a meeting and always completed assigned work. James actively participated in his recovery and restoration. This was an important season in his life and he pressed into the change process completely and gave a 100% effort. He started with a bit of a wobble, made the necessary adjustments along the way, and finished strong. Through the process of change, James accepted a new identity— that of a renewed and transformed husband, a father who is present, and a fellow warrior within a band of brothers.

Tonight, as I write this observation, the group that met every Monday for the past year gathered for the last time and a stage of James' journey officially ended. From my experience of co-leading this group, I gained a better understanding of what is required to finish well and to finish strong, and James Craft provided that example. When prompted, James speaks of the hours each week spent pouring over the treatment and restoration material. He completed the readings and the exercises, the self-reflections, difficult letters, and heartbreaking conversations. He went deep to discover the source of the pain and wounds that drove the coping behaviors that kept him isolated and alone. James was fearless in his pursuit of clarity and understanding and reconciliation with his wife and children.

James refused to give labels from his past the power to define his future, and did the difficult work required for change. Through the experience, James gained a deeper understanding of who God has called him to be: A man of honor and integrity who is willing to do the hard work and finish strong.

Chapter 5

THE NOT SO GREAT WIZARD

Jesus helped me see clearly that in order to live, love, and forgive empathetically, I must be willing to give Him all in exchange for everything.

Like many Americans, I grew up watching *The Wizard of Oz*. I loved the black and white scene with Dorothy and Toto as they get swept up in a tornado. Her house flies through the air and lands safely back on the ground. But the awesome part is when she opens the door. The boring black and white world she had always known bursts into a Technicolor adventure in the land of Oz. Dorothy embarks on a quest to find the wizard who can get her back home to Kansas. I was totally intrigued by the great wizard. At first, I was overwhelmed by the thought of his greatness and power, but then, in the midst of the intense exchange between Dorothy and the wizard, Toto runs over and pulls back the curtain to expose an ordinary man who was merely pushing buttons, pulling levers, and speaking in a microphone. This greater–than–life personality turns out to be a facade.

CHAPTER 5 – THE NOT SO GREAT WIZARD

I relate to that not-so-great-wizard in my dysfunction. Someone asked me recently to describe the difference between my life currently and how I functioned in the past. I shared with them that in the past, I felt a little like that ordinary man trying to push all the buttons and keep the facade going. Upfront, I was confident, strong, and knew where I was going, but as I described previously, I was masking great woundedness beneath. Ultimately, however, God allowed the curtain to be pulled to the side to expose the broken, insecure man I really was. I became a master at living my life with different compartments. It was very natural for me to organize my life in such a way. I can't remember ever doing it any differently. I had a compartment for husband, dad, friend, pastor, addict, and, eventually, one for an affair. You see, God never intended for me, or anyone for that matter, to construct such a massive conglomerate of isolated areas in one soul. His desire is for all of us to live life free in Him, and be fully present no matter who we are with or what we are doing. These compartments demanded a great deal of my energy and focus because I had to create a different persona for each one to hide behind and cover the fear and insecurity.

God loved me too much to leave me the way I was, so He allowed my safety mechanism to be blown up, forcing me to live within one compartment…health! It is a whole new world to live present with my loved ones and have nothing, and I mean nothing, to hide. My capacity and functionality as a human being has been tripled due to the fact that I now put all my energies into living this pure, honest life with God and others. My friend, that is what awaits all of us when we live in freedom; we essentially operate the way our Father intended when He created us. This means that I have to choose daily, just as Christ encourages us in Luke 9:23:

Then he said to them all: "Whoever wants to be my disciple must deny themselves and take up their cross daily and follow me."

The key word is "daily," meaning I must wake up each day and take an assessment of my life with the leading of the Holy Spirit; surrender my fleshly tendencies; and realize that life happens, trials come, and triggers are everywhere. I must be willing to face the hard stuff on this journey with Christ and do it in my skin, remembering I only have one life to live.

The antithesis of open and healthy living is one that I know all too well. I am speaking very genuinely when I say that living with compartments is a monumental disaster waiting to happen. My previous life was much like a Coke bottle that had been shaken violently for minutes. The pressure on the inside was hardly containable. When you spend most of your life trying to keep the lid on, you lose a great deal of hope in the process. I didn't have the tools I now have for ongoing healthy living. The longer I functioned in isolation and addiction to pornography, the more these sub-par medications became less than enough to cope with the pain, and I eventually lost hope for my very life.

All the dreams that were birthed in my heart began to die and my strength to carry on was gone. I started to frantically push all the buttons and pull all the levers behind that curtain, not having any energy left for much of anything else. I essentially opened my already fragmented life to the deep lies and deception of the enemy. In doing so, I also opened my loved ones to the same depravity. I had thoughts like, *Who cares anymore? You've blown it this bad, you can't get any worse. You've always been a failure.* Or, *It would be better if you weren't here on earth to bring shame to yourself and your family.* I couldn't sleep at night, and I had difficulty concentrating during the day. The enemy of my soul kept pushing his bony finger into the open wounds of my life, and I kept running in fear, which created more and more facades and compartments. My friend, that is not fertile ground for loving your wife and family the way God intended them to be covered and cared for.

My life finally came to an end, or you could say I was given a restart. I equate it to being in full cardiac arrest. The Lord basically stuck a life–saving defibrillator right on my chest that sent an electrical charge straight to my heart, quite frankly just before it was too late. After coming clean in full repentance for the affair and the porn addiction, God was able to start the renovation of my life. I didn't realize how many different compartments or "rooms" I had in my soul until I had removed the debris that was piled up. I was a hoarder of pain and shame. When I was finally faced with allowing the demolition to take place, I could see how much work lay before me. It felt a little like one of those renovation shows where they start with a run–down house, tear it down by ripping out walls, beams, and foundations, then rebuild it from the ground up. When you are standing in the middle of what looks like tornado debris, but finally have the correct vision for the God–ordained finished product, you have to make some really hard decisions.

I decided that I would not use anything but honesty and vulnerability to deal with the pain that came my way, a posturing that, quite simply, puts me continually at the feet of Jesus. I know it may be confusing to some regarding what my pornography addiction entailed. I didn't even realize it was an addiction until I was in the first stages of therapy. After walking through the restoration process, I saw that my cycle of relapse, which was monthly or weekly when stress was really heightened, was, in fact, an addictive cycle. This was a cycle that I unknowingly put my family through each and every time I relapsed.

This truth obliterates the notion that there is no harm in keeping a destructive behavior a secret and naively thinking you're protecting your loved ones. One way or another, it's going to do damage to others around you. I realize that it was something I tried to end many times in my life and couldn't until I dealt with the hurt and fear that was driving the behavior. I needed the tools and accountability to sustain that freedom. I had to be honest with myself and others about this very deep pit of despair that I couldn't get out of alone or overnight.

I decided to live out the truth that I would never be a good husband until I embraced that I am a beloved son of my Heavenly Father; I would never be a good dad until I was a loving and sacrificial husband to my wife; and I could never be used effectively of the Lord outside my family until all those things were functioning in a healthy manner. In order to do this, I had to submit to the process and work in the correct order being laid out before me by Dr. Ted. I had to first concentrate on my healing, then I focused on seeing Teri and I heal together from this place of health. After our marriage regained strength and stability, Teri and I could focus on our girls and see our family whole. Attempting to fix my family first would have caused more damage. This is where I am blessed beyond description to have a wife and family that gave great grace and patiently trusted in the Lord to do what He does best. Taking the slow and hard road allowed God's healing power to work through me, then to work in our marriage, and eventually to work safely into our family to break the generational issues that existed.

I decided to forgive and forgive again. Each day I had to remind myself of how much I have been forgiven. Knowing that God had forgiven me and loved me through my darkest hours helped me keep the correct focus, that I was called to forgive those who hurt me in my past and present, as well as learn to forgive myself. I had the manifest evidence before me of what can happen in a person's life when unforgiveness has had time to fester and distort, leaving only a hard heart and a bitter soul. So, I had to choose every day to extend forgiveness, the very thing Jesus is so faithful in demonstrating to those who He loves and died for. I had to come to grips with the fact that it was working through the process of forgiveness toward others, as well as laying down my guilt and shame from my own hurtful decisions that would be one of the hardest tasks of all. I was reminded often of Luke 7:36–50, a passage of Scripture I studied and taught from many times.

When one of the Pharisees invited Jesus to have dinner with him, he went to the Pharisee's house and reclined at the table. A woman in that town who lived a sinful life learned that Jesus was eating at the Pharisee's house, so she came there with an alabaster jar of perfume. As she stood behind him at his feet weeping, she began to wet his feet with her tears. Then she wiped them with her hair, kissed them and poured perfume on them. When the Pharisee who had invited him saw this, he said to himself, "If this man were a prophet, he would know who is touching him and what kind of woman she is—that she is a sinner."

Jesus answered him, "Simon, I have something to tell you."

"Tell me, teacher," he said.

"Two people owed money to a certain moneylender. One owed him five hundred denarii, and the other fifty. Neither of them had the money to pay him back, so he forgave the debts of both. Now which of them will love him more?"

Simon replied, "I suppose the one who had the bigger debt forgiven."

"You have judged correctly," Jesus said.

Then he turned toward the woman and said to Simon, "Do you see this woman? I came into your house. You did not give me any water for my feet, but she wet my feet with her tears and wiped them with her hair. You did not give me a kiss, but this woman, from the time I entered, has not stopped kissing my feet. You did not put oil on my head, but she has poured perfume on my feet. Therefore, I tell you, her many sins have been forgiven—as her great love has shown. But whoever has been forgiven little loves little."

Then Jesus said to her, "Your sins are forgiven."

The other guests began to say among themselves, "Who is this who even forgives sins?"

Jesus said to the woman, "Your faith has saved you; go in peace."

I have always been struck by this account of Jesus and His response to the Pharisee's inquisition of the forgiven woman, but in my darkest moments of transformation I could relate with every fabric of my being. It was as if I could see the scene before me and hear Jesus' tender, but firm voice saying, "Simon, do you see this precious person?" On the outside, that question was kind of obvious. I can picture Simon saying, "Well…yes, I can see her right here in front of me with my own two eyes." But Jesus wasn't checking his vision. He was asking a deeper question. He was inquiring if Simon could see his own humanity in terms of his need of forgiveness as much as hers. Jesus was asking him, "Do you see this woman, or do you see only the failure, the sinner, and her past when you look at her?" The very question Jesus was presenting was piercing right to the heart of Simon's potential for an empathetic response. The heartbreaking answer was that Simon couldn't see this woman as Jesus did, for he only saw her as she was. Jesus saw her for who she could become in Him. This is the Savior that rescued and forgave this woman, and it was the same Savior who was pulling me out of my pit of sin and despair. You see, Jesus placed Himself between His beloved and her accuser by asking Simon this question, yet, all the while keeping His eyes fixed on the one He loved. The one who had opened her heart wide to Him, even in her broken state of existence.

The Message translation communicates this perfectly (verse 44): "Then turning to the woman, but speaking to Simon, he said, "Do you see this woman?" He firmly made the declaration that if Simon wanted to effectively see this woman, he'd have to look through Him to do it. It is the thought of those eyes of love transfixed upon the weary soul that uplifted me time and time again to forgive and forgive again, knowing that, (verse 47) "therefore, I tell you, her many sins have been forgiven—as her great love has shown. But whoever has been forgiven little loves little." The fact remains, we all need a lot of forgiving in our lifetime, both for our acts of sin and as a demonstration extended outward toward those who have hurt us. Jesus helped me see clearly that in order to live, love, and forgive empathetically, I must be willing to give Him all in exchange for everything.

I decided that when I felt myself wanting to construct a wall or compartmentalize any area of my life, I would tell someone in my accountability circle, even if it seemed small. I had to do this often at first, but as I started to see health enter my life and was open and honest with my family, it became the norm to live in my skin. It became a second language in our family. We were able to communicate with one another the challenges that were taking place. Our family started to see each other as allies rather than enemies. Teri and I had to practice a deeper level of honesty and transparency every day.

In the very early stages of recovery, when I relapsed, I had to share that with Teri within the first twenty-four hours. We had a safety plan established for Teri and the girls, so when relapse occurred, I had to age appropriately confess to the family and sleep on the floor for up to two weeks. This was important for my girls to see, because even Dad had consequence for his actions. I'm incredibly thankful to the Lord for this safety plan, the Pure Desire program, and, most importantly, His power to heal, because together they brought freedom from my addiction within ninety days. I was then charged with walking in freedom by allowing the re-patterning to take place. I communicated to my wife and reached out to my small group of guys when I was faced with challenges or failure. In the past, I would never have done that. I finally started to see my value in life. As I opened my heart up to my Father, those compartments started to crumble and security started to rise.

I decided to own what was mine and let God do what He wanted in others in His timing. I repented genuinely for the damage my sinful choices had caused others in my life. I was also counseled that I could only take responsibility for the things I had done, not the things that people held onto from their own pasts and projected toward me in their anger. I learned to be honest and upfront in confessing what I had done wrong, ask for forgiveness, and allow healthy conversations to take place. But I couldn't force others to pursue health and forgiveness in my timing; that was up to God. I realized God was requiring out of me humility, honesty, transparency, and a willingness to do what was right. This included acknowledging that every person is on his or her own journey. Learning to extend love when things aren't resolved is the grace–filled way Christ would have me live in response to that same grace He was giving to me.

I decided, with the power of the Holy Spirit in me, that fear would no longer rule my life and I would not give the enemy a foothold by believing his lies anymore. This was one of the greatest challenges I faced. For most of my life, I believed the lies that the enemy told me each and every day. Those lies became the truth by which I measured situations and eventually distorted every behavior that came from that place of deception. I had to go back and discover God's heart for me when He created me in my mother's womb. I had to rediscover the promises that the Lord established in my life and apply them back into the DNA of my person. "Such love has no fear, because perfect love expels all fear. If we are afraid, it is for fear of punishment, and this shows that we have not fully experienced His perfect love" 1 John 4:18 (NLT). This daily decision required some serious warfare and a relentless commitment to trust the Lord's leading through His Word. A great quote by Nelson Mandela says it all, "I learned that courage was not the absence of fear, but the triumph over it. The brave man is not he who does not feel afraid, but he who conquers that fear."[4]

I decided to accept the new information we were learning, thereby replacing the old misguided information that previously pervaded my thoughts. As I mentioned earlier, it took thirty years to get into this deep pit of despair, so I had to patiently and daily learn a new way of living. My Pure Desire material became my manual on how to live life. I poured myself into my daily homework and God's Word. I allowed these times to reshape my thinking about myself and how I walked through life. Without these tools, I would continue to revert back to my default that was established as my safety mechanism from my childhood.

After walking through the healing process with Teri and the girls for about nine months, I wrote this journal entry that I think clearly communicates the God–ordained process that allowed the rebuilding in my life:

JANUARY 2, 2014

Wow! We now have made it to the New Year! I know many people would assume that we are more than happy to leave 2013 behind us because it was the worst year of our lives. I would categorize it more accurately as the most challenging year of our lives, but also the most profoundly transformative at the same time. Isn't it in those types of environments that the Lord often does His greatest work? Isn't it in those times when we are faced with the impossible or have come to the end of ourselves and it seems like a hopeless mess. Just about the

---

4   The Independent, "Nelson Mandela: 11 Inspirational Quotes to Live Your Life By" http://www.independent.co.uk/news/world/nelson-mandela-10-inspirational-quotes-to-live-your-life-by-8988290.html?action=gallery (accessed Mar. 19, 2015).

moment we are ready to call it quits, we push in against all odds and discover a facet of God we had never experienced before. There are so many lessons our family has learned, but I am coming to really see that it only makes us stronger in the Lord. As I look back at the journal entries from the past, I can see how I desperately wanted healing for myself, and for my family. I didn't know what that would look like, but it was a deep desire of my heart. It's amazing how desperate you can become when you want something you know you need, but don't know how to get it.

My life these past nine months has been like a bowl of sticky spaghetti, all tangled up in a gigantic mess. Metaphorically speaking, I had to daily take one noodle at a time and allow it become unraveled with the help of the Holy Spirit. Was it easy? No, but it was so incredibly worth it. Am I finished? Not until I am with the Lord in Heaven will I be finished growing, learning, responding, and healing in one way or another. It's what Jesus has called us to on this planet. I do know without a doubt that this journey takes a whole lot of patience and humility knowing it's not going to happen overnight.

It reminds me of a time when my dad took me fishing at the Ventura Pier. After casting out my line, I waited and waited and waited. I decided to check my line by pulling on it to see what was on the end. As I started to reel it in, it suddenly stopped. My first thought was that I had the biggest and greatest catch on the end of my line. My mind started to go crazy with thoughts like, "This was going to end up on the front page of the Star Free Press." My dad came over to help me reel in whatever was pulling at the end of my line. As we started to wind the reel with anticipation mounting after each click, click, click, we noticed that it was getting heavier and heavier. Finally, the end of the line broke through the water and I looked down to see a huge pile of seaweed connected to it. We pulled it in and I started to clean off the seaweed and I noticed something. There was a weight and a line connected to it. That line ran all the way back into the water. So, being the inquisitive and energetic boy that I was, I started to pull on it excitedly to see what would appear. It must have taken me more then ten minutes to pull that line in, but I was determined. I finally got toward the end and noticed a huge ball of tangled line with something hanging beneath that looked like a long stick. I wanted to see what this was so I continued to pull it in and noticed it was a deep–sea fishing pole with the end snapped off. "Wow," I thought to myself, "someone must have caught something really big and it snapped the end right off." My only other thought was…"This pole is mine!"

I made the decision right then and there that I was going to untangle that mess, polish the pole, and repair the end; it would be my very own pole. I can only imagine what I looked like that day going home. I carried an enormous pile of fishing line and a broken fishing pole, all with a huge smile on my face. I remember spending the next month on my parents' porch untangling that unruly ball of fishing line. I knew I wouldn't be able to have a clean and working pole unless I took the time to untangle the mess. I eventually accomplished my goal. The line was straight, back on the reel, and ready to be used. I cleaned up the pole, put on a new end, and I was ready to go.

I relate to this story with my very life. That pole was lying on the bottom of the ocean floor, a tangled mess, never to be used again. Some little boy connected with it, pulled it up, and took the time to unravel the line and bring it back to the way it was supposed to be. I know whole–heartedly that I was at the bottom of the ocean of hopelessness—lost, broken, and a tangled, unruly mess. The Lord has graciously and lovingly taken the time to untangle my mess of compartments, polish me up, and restore my broken pieces, so that someday I can be used for His glory once again.

I know there are many who can relate to this story of mine in one way or another. It could be that you are feeling a little like that not-so-great-wizard pushing all the buttons, hoping you can keep it all going, or you may relate to the feeling of having your life twisted and bound up like an endless bowl of sticky spaghetti. Regardless of which describes you, we, as the children of God, were not created to live the rest of our lives on the bottom of a dark and desolate ocean floor, never to be used again. Our Heavenly Father has so lovingly extended a line of hope to latch onto our lives in an attempt to reel us inward toward the promises awaiting each and every one of us in Him.

If I think back on a great portion of my life, I realize now that I kept kicking and fighting to survive, not comprehending that the things that I thought were sustaining me were the very things that were drowning and killing me. My masks and facades were suffocating me. I mistakenly believed that God wanted me to stay at the bottom of that ocean floor for all I had done. Shame blinded me from the truth that was always right in front of me. Even though the line of hope kept rubbing against me, I never thought I was good enough to grab hold of it. All the while, my Jesus had His arms open wide, welcoming me into His warm embrace of forgiveness and love. I understand now that my life, though difficult in its formative years, didn't just happen by accident, but has been orchestrated by a God who has loved me more than the words of these pages can describe. The path I chose to walk in life didn't surprise Him. Being the omniscient Lord that He is, He stood patiently waiting for me to come out of captivity and walk the path He paved for me. He does the same for you.

Let Jeremiah 29 (The Message) be a wonderful reminder of what awaits all of us in Christ Jesus.

As soon as Babylon's seventy years are up and not a day before, I'll show up and take care of you as I promised and bring you back home. I know what I'm doing. I have it all planned out—plans to take care of you, not abandon you, plans to give you the future you hope for. When you call on me, when you come and pray to me, I'll listen. When you come looking for me, you'll find me. Yes, when you get serious about finding me and want it more than anything else, I'll make sure you won't be disappointed.

Chapter 6
I MET GOD
IN THE MARGINS

God stands in the margins of our lives,
leading us back and forth across the page of our existence.

I was one of those kids who drew outside the lines. I knew there were margins on the paper, but for some reason my work often bled into that off–limits, white space. My teacher did not approve. I asked her one day, "Why do I have to stay in the margins and not use all of my paper?" My teacher told me that margins make it easier for people to read and gives her room to write how well I was doing. That stuck with me through school, but something broke down when it came to the functionality of my life. Margins became space to fill rather than space to receive.

My life became all about running as fast as I could. I lived life to the extreme. I pushed to the front of the line in sports. I pushed to the top of the social ladder. I pushed ahead in ministry with zeal. I ran flat out sprinting until I hit a wall. And I didn't just hit the wall; I smashed into it, and the wall smacked me back. Laying sprawled out on the pavement, out of breath, it became obvious that this life sprint wasn't God's plan for me, and it's not His plan for you.

Through this reconstruction of my life, I began to see that God stands in the margins of our lives, leading us back and forth across the page of our existence. The Lord desires that we run our individual race with great purpose and vision, but we are called to pause in the margins to hear our Father speak to us, give Him our praise, and listen carefully to His instruction for what lies ahead. I discovered in my newfound quiet and intimate times with the Lord that you simply can't receive the life–giving direction that awaits you in the margins if you are sprinting to the next line to continue the story in your own strength. It's not an option, my friend, we must stop and receive—even if the thought of stopping scares you. Please let Isaiah 40:31 (**NKJV**) be an encouragement to you.

> *But those who wait on the Lord*
> *Shall renew their strength;*
> *They shall mount up with wings like eagles,*
> *They shall run and not be weary,*
> *They shall walk and not faint.*

This portion of Scripture is about trusting God and allowing Him full rein of your life. It's about surrender. This posture leads to spiritual, physical, and emotional victory and transformation. It comes from slowing down long enough to engage with the One who has the power to transform. The verses preceding 31 help us understand that God is who He says He is, and that we need Him to meet our every need.

Have you not known?
Have you not heard?
The everlasting God, the Lord,
The Creator of the ends of the earth, neither faints nor is weary.
His understanding is unsearchable.
He gives power to the weak,
and to those who have no might He increases strength,
even the youths shall faint and be weary,
And the young men shall utterly fall...

And the prescription for those of us who are running so hard and fast, who have gotten tired and weary, who have used up the margins and are fainting under the weight of life is simply this, go back to verse 31...and repeat...daily.

A NEW BEGINNING

I've always been intrigued by things that go fast. All through my life I competed in track and field and played football, but running an all–out race has always been my favorite activity. In today's world, you don't have to go too far to find people who are adrenaline junkies. On the outside, it may seem as if most of them are just in it for the thrill of it all, which keeps pushing them to go further and further, forsaking all for the ultimate rush. I believe many, like my old self, are not so much looking for a thrill, but running from (or toward) something so hard, that the rush becomes a mechanism of distraction, protection, and self–medicating, more than an end.

When I worked as the National Youth Director for the Foursquare denomination, I was given the opportunity by a wealthy businessman in Washington State to visit a NHRA drag racing competition as a possible evangelistic outreach tool. A fellow pastor and I went to the Las Vegas Motor Speedway to meet some teams and their owners to see what it was all about. When we arrived at the speedway, I couldn't believe what I saw. There were thousands and thousands of people as far as the eye could see. As we walked around, we saw the attention to detail each team put into their cars for the race. Every bolt, belt, and screw was checked. Each car was a masterpiece of science, technology, and speed.

We were invited to go to the starting line to watch two Top Fuel dragsters race head–to–head. The host gave us a pair of headphones to protect our ears and yelled, "Follow me!" above the noise of the engines. My heart raced as we walked across the track and stood near the starting line. They rolled the two dragsters up to the line and made all the final adjustments to the car and driver. The host gave us a few words of instruction and warning as the dragsters rolled off a short distance down the track to get ready for the start. He yelled the instruction, "Make sure to stand still and breathe through your mouth." I didn't have a clue what he was talking about, but I was going to heed his every word.

The starting light flashed. The two dragsters fired off 14,000 horsepower between the two of them and burned thirty gallons of nitromethane fuel to send them flying down the track on the quarter mile stretch at speeds over 330 mph in 4.4 seconds… now that was fast. After the race, I realized why the host told us to stand still and breathe through our mouths. When all the horsepower fired off, my feet had vibrated back over eight inches, and the inside of my nose burned from the nitromethane fuel burned off by the dragsters.

What an experience! My pastor friend and I were amazed by the power, speed, and science that went into each race. There was no room for error, seeing as that would be the difference between a win or a loss, or even life and death for the driver. The pit crew had to make sure everything was checked and checked again post–race so that they could experience victory at the finish line in the future. We have all seen videos of out–of–control dragsters going down the track, which typically ended up in a fireball of destruction.

The image of a fireball careening down the track was my life leading up to this recovery season. I was running so hard from my pain while trying to achieve the next best thing that I rarely experienced God's peace in my life. It seems obvious that I'd realize a crash was imminent and I'd hurt those I loved the most, but my mindset was so performance–based that all I could see was the need to reach the next goal.

I found my acceptance and affirmation in the sheer craziness of striving. Ultimately, this track was a dead end. The bottom line is that my pace was something I wanted to control, but could never come to grips with how. I mentioned in the last chapter that during my recovery and restoration, my life resembled one of those renovation shows where they rip the house apart down to the foundation and build a new one from the ground up. This is really what was going on beneath the surface as I was learning how to slow down long enough to commune with God and let Him heal my wounds—wounds that had become destructive not only to me but also to so many precious people as well.

In most of my chaotic life, I drove so hard and so fast that I missed God speaking to me about me. It was like driving down the freeway at eighty miles an hour while sticking my head out the window and trying to have a conversation with the person in the passenger seat. That's not the best environment for clear communication, to say the least. Running at this breakneck speed and trying to accomplish the next big project, while running from the lies of my past, drove me deeper into the pornography addiction, which I used to cope with the exhaustion and shame that had built up in my life. The harder I drove, the more isolated I became. The more I did, the less I had. I kept running away from the pain, rejection, and anger I had in life, and I ran right past God. The difficulty for those in my family was that most of the time I was cheerful, energetic, and patient, but when stress, rejection, shame, or fatigue kicked in, the cycle drove me into isolation, medication, anger, and then retaliation. This lifestyle drove everyone involved into deeper levels of confusion and fear. All while the Lord waited patiently in the margins for me to stop long enough for Him to sing His love song over the places of my hopelessness, fear, shame, and pain…until one day when God allowed another very needed crash in my life.

It was a Saturday morning in mid-July 2013, a few difficult months into my recovery and family restoration. I started to act agitated and short with my family. Teri knew something was wrong. She was being trained in all the same recovery techniques and methods that I was and knew what to look for when I was in a cycle. She came into the bedroom where I was and asked me point blank, "Did you relapse with pornography?"

I didn't give her an answer; all I did was jump to my feet and yell at the top of my voice, "I'm done!" I ran out of the house and up the street with no place in mind. When I said I was done, I meant it. I was done running and trying to do this on my own and in my own strength. *But where do I go?* I'd never stopped long enough in my life to know what to do when you've come to the end.

I had relapsed the day before, and when Teri asked me, I was done failing God in this way. I was done hurting her in this way. I hit rock bottom, even lower than the day I was exposed, because now I was accountable and I had nowhere to turn... but up. I ran to an open parking lot, sat down on the corner and cried so violently I thought my insides were coming out. I think it was a combination of a breakdown and deliverance all in one. After crying for almost an hour, memories of my childhood that I had repressed came to the surface, and I could sense the Lord's hand in what was happening. It was like the anger was being brought to the surface and peeled away like a Band–Aid. It hurt; it was actually excruciating, but at the same time it felt right— like being repaired after a life–saving surgery.

Teri found me sitting in the parking lot. She calmly looked me in the eyes and said, "God's got this, James," and we walked home. After that meltdown, we came together as a family and prayed over each other. Teri and I didn't hide that I had a rough morning because, let's face it, the kids could tell Dad wasn't looking his finest with his swollen, red eyes. We talked with the kids about how sometimes you have good days, and sometimes you have days that you need a little help from your loved ones and a whole lot of help from Jesus. A lot of Christ–centered healing took place that day. The enemy had tried again to destroy our family. It was painfully profound.

I called Dr. Ted and shared with him that I had relapsed and didn't tell him or Teri right away, and how that conflict had thrown me into what seemed like some kind of mental and spiritual meltdown. After sharing everything that had happened, he started cheering on the other end of the phone. I could feel my blood pressure rising. His jubilation over what I was saying angered me. *Sure a lot of great stuff happened, but he didn't have to be so excited about it,* I thought. At that moment I'd had enough, so I yelled, "Why are you celebrating in my time of pain?" Dr. Ted calmly responded,

"James, you've finally come to the end of yourself. Let's start rebuilding your life together." There was a long, silent pause, but then relief washed over me through his words. I knew I wasn't alone and that there was hope for complete freedom.

After that breakdown day in July, something happened in me that I had never experienced before. I started to slow down, because honestly, I didn't have anything to outrun. Teri and I processed with Dr. Ted and Diane regarding what had happened that day, what triggered me in the first place, and how to properly deal with the memories that came to the surface through the experience. I started to listen, really listen, because I didn't have the noise of despair blaring in my ears. I had an encounter with my Heavenly Father because time essentially stood still long enough for me to recognize I was out of control. I learned the rhythm of my Father, and that required me to take time to pause in the margins of life.

If you are anything like I was, you won't experience freedom from addiction, anger, shame, fear, or resentment unless you take the time to pause, get real with what's going on inside, and allow yourself to have an encounter with the Author of your love story. It's an amazing thing when you start to walk contemplatively with the Lord. Even nature became more vivid and beautiful when I slowed down. The sunset on a summer evening, the fragrance of the night air, and the unique fingerprint of God's creation displayed all around were ways He was communicating to me moment by moment. The smiles and laughter of my wife and children brought me to tears in an instant, filling my soul with overwhelming gratitude and thankfulness. I began to hear the echo of the Lord's love and the firm voice of warning that was guarding me from dangers I couldn't even see yet.

I'm reminded of one of the best surfing days I ever had. We were living in eastern San Francisco Bay area while I was youth pastoring in Danville, California. I had grown up in Southern California where we rarely got the size surf I was adjusting to in Northern California. Let's just say it was a big, mean, cold wave in NorCal. After a near–death experience that happened just a week prior, where I almost drowned when the force of the waves repeatedly held me under the water, I got wise and asked a friend who had grown up as a big wave surfer in Hawaii if he could help me out.

We arrived at the beach before the sun came up, or what we called, "dawn patrol." The air was moist and cold as we put on our wetsuits beside the road. What he asked me to do next was different from any of my previous surfing experiences. We got ready, grabbed our boards, and then sat on the beach for 20 minutes. Yep, we just sat there and watched as the sun rose and numerous sets of waves rolled in. He explained to me, "You need to watch the rhythm of the sets, see where you can enter, and look for the channels (where the water goes back out after the waves come crashing in). You'll use half the energy." I kept thinking to myself, *I sure wish I would've had this information last week when I almost died.* After twenty minutes of observing where each channel was, we picked up our boards and paddled right out to the lineup. That was one of the best days of surfing I've ever had. Instead of killing myself trying to get out into the lineup, I allowed the movement of water to do the work for me.

I understand now that's just what the Lord allows us to do when we come away with Him. He teaches us His loving ways and makes us aware of unseen dangers. He reminds us that He is for us, and the present pressures we face in life are subject to His power if we give Him that control.

But in that coming day **no weapon** *turned against you will*

succeed. You will silence every voice raised up to accuse you.
These benefits are enjoyed by the servants of the Lord; their
vindication will come from me. I, the Lord, have spoken!
Isaiah 54:17 (NLT)

My friend, I realize we live in a fast–paced world. I understand completely that it takes a lot of time, effort, and energy to succeed in the ever–changing and evolving technological marketplaces. I empathize deeply with pastors and ministers who are trying to keep up with the growing demands of their parishioners, while simultaneously staying relevant and up to date for the next generation of families in this difficult economy. I know how it feels as a parent to think that if your child isn't in all the extracurricular classes and year round athletic teams that you are somehow letting them down and stunting their future. But the real truth is that God created the margins in our lives for a reason, and the most important reason is to be touched by Him so we can touch our world.

A new command I give you: Love one another. As I have loved
you, so you must love one another. By this everyone will know
that you are my disciples, if you love one another.
John 13:34–35

It's very hard to give transforming love away unless you are being transformed by that same love, and it's near impossible to be transformed unless you are taking time to learn of and receive that love in close–range communication with Love Himself. Our marriages, our families, the next generation, those in need of hope, and the weary souls existing all around us on a daily basis are worthy of the kind of love God has for them, not our human "B" version. It is a surreal thing to live in rhythm with the Lord in such a way that all your relationships are positively affected by the sacred exchange of His transformative love to you and through you. It is easy to point upward and say, "To Him be all the glory," and mean it with your whole heart when peace lives in you and you know it's not of your making. It directs your attention heavenward on a moment–by–moment basis and you fight against anything that gets in the way of that vital connection point.

The following are a few of the practical tools Teri and I have incorporated into our lives to protect our margins and create environments that are conductive to a more paced and contemplative walk with the Lord:

The 24 hour rule. We have mutually made a commitment to help each other stay committed to using the rhythm of a day, or twenty–four hours, to help us respond to, instead of react to, situations that come our way. When we get a stressful phone call regarding business matters, a person makes an unkind comment and we want to immediately write "that" email in response, or we are faced with a situation that requires us to make a change or decision, we use this rule to help us take it to the Lord and hear His heart about the situation. Every time we have opted to wait on the Lord instead of react, He has brought great clarity, peace, and direction. There have even been many times that He has spoken to our hearts to wait longer before deciding or responding, and He has been spot on every time. Teri and I have laughed a few times after the Lord miraculously worked out a situation when we waited the twenty–four hour period and said to one another, "Why has it taken us this long to figure this one out?"

Taking long walks. We try to walk together as much as we can. These moments have been impactful for the entire twenty-two years of our marriage. Now, we use our walks, not only for processing life situations, but for prayer and praise as well. There are times we just talk of the goodness of the Lord, pray about situations that are pressing, and even walk in silence together. The other component of this practical tool is that we walk by ourselves as well. I can say without a doubt that some of my most profound moments with the Lord have been when I walked the hills near our home in the early mornings or late afternoons and just talked with and listened to my Father God.

Reading the Word of God for the purpose of knowing Him better. Of course, I still study the Word and do directed devotions, but I have incorporated times with the Lord that I just read, wait, and listen…read, wait and listen for no other purpose, but to know the Lord more fully and hear His heart for me. I had gotten to the point that I was preparing so many teachings a week that my reading became more textbook–like. When the world as I knew it blew up and I had no teachings to prepare for, God got real with me about my motivation and application of absorbing His Word.

Priorities. Our top priority is Jesus, and our family values come next. Everything else is filtered through that lens. In my dysfunction, I had gotten my priorities out of order. There is nothing like almost losing everything that is dear to you and watching your family suffer under the weight of your unhealthy choices to help you re–prioritize and correct back to Jesus' best. Now, we stay true to the Lord first and foremost. This goes back to waiting and listening before acting. Then, we filter any decision through our established family values that our girls helped create. It's non-negotiable.

Remembering that I have nothing to prove and that my best contribution in life will be a free and pure relationship with my Father in Heaven. This may or may not make sense to some reading this book, but when you have lived most of your life with a performance based mindset (that mindset that kept me constantly going and driving so hard), to walk in peace with the Lord is like being cured of cancer. He holds my destiny and I only need to get my cues and my sense of worth and value from Him and walk in freedom. Anything that comes from that foundational place will be light years ahead of any effort I make in my own strength, especially where my loved ones are concerned.

Long, Deep Breaths. I find myself taking long, deep breaths now. I understand in a physiological sense it is beneficial to saturate my brain with oxygen, especially when I get stressed and my breathing pattern shortens. But, it is also a tool to help me relax and once again focus my attention back on the Lord. One of our daughters has a severe allergy to peanuts. It has caused her to panic in situations when she is in public and peanuts are present, even if they are out of her range. We've taught her to take eight deep breaths when she feels out of control, and then talk to Jesus and ask Him to bring her peace. It has helped her a great deal. She will come home and tell us how these tools helped her overcome fear about a situation at school or at a friend's house.

This is what the Sovereign Lord, the Holy One of Israel, says:
"Only in returning to me and resting in me will you be saved.
In quietness and confidence is your strength."
Isaiah 30:15 (NLT)

I've always loved King David; to read of His fearless conquests and steadfast leadership amidst trials has continually inspired me. But, it's the quieter and more contemplative side of David that I am impressed with these days. You can't go too far into any Psalm he penned and not hear his heart on rest and worship, and his longing to communicate with the Lord with every breath and with all his focus. My friend, that kind of commitment takes time, not the running kind of time, but the quiet, margin kind of time. That kind of life is all about surrender. I find great comfort in Psalms 23. It's all about trust, provision, proximity…and pace. I read it almost daily as a reminder of my Shepherd's great love for me, and my dependence on Him.

PSALM 23 (NLT)
A psalm of David

The Lord is my shepherd;
I have all that I need.
He lets me rest in green meadows;
he leads me beside peaceful streams.
He renews my strength.
He guides me along right paths,
bringing honor to his name.
Even when I walk
through the darkest valley,
I will not be afraid,

for you are close beside me.
Your rod and your staff
protect and comfort me.
You prepare a feast for me
in the presence of my enemies.
You honor me by anointing my head with oil.
My cup overflows with blessings.
Surely your goodness and unfailing love will pursue
me all the days of my life,
and I will live in the house of the Lord
forever.

When our trust, proximity to the Lord, and pace are off, so are
our lives. I have come to grips with the fact that my previous
choice to stay in that place of frenzied chaos was detrimental
to those around me. I've written this testimony to speak of the
hope found in Jesus, but also to give a warning to any reader who
may be thinking they can outlive the pain and woundedness that
drives a crazy, over-paced lifestyle. You can't, and you won't.
There is a choice; make it!

I have told you all this so that you may have peace in me. Here
on earth you will have many trials and sorrows. But take heart,
because I have overcome the world.
John 16:33 (NLT)

Chapter 7
FINISHING STRONG

I started my life as a wounded boy, and, from the ashes, Jesus refined a broken man into a disciple.

"It's not how you start the race, it's how you finish." I've heard that all my life. After all we've gone through on this new journey individually, as a married couple, and as a family, I now personally identify with this statement as if it was tattooed on my arm.

You may remember from past chapters that I spent many years competing in track and field. I learned early on that if you stepped out on the racetrack thinking you were going to lose, you typically did. But, if you stepped out onto the track positively focused and determined, you almost always accomplished more than you thought possible. There is, however, a very distinct hazard in running as fast as you can with others all around you, and that, my friend, is tripping and falling. I have seen many people tragically fall during their races, and I have a few pretty good face–plant stories of my own. But, in the world of track and field, very few top the comeback story of Heather Dorniden.

Heather was an 800–meter runner for the University of Minnesota. She rewrote the record books at her school and beyond, not so much with a record time, but with her heart. It's not her athletic prowess that impressed so many worldwide, but her determination and resilience in finishing one amazing race that took place in the final heat of the 600 meters at the Big Ten Indoor Track Championships in 2008.

Heather was the clear favorite to win the heat. The gun went off and she lunged forward with all the other competitors, something she'd done hundreds, if not thousands, of times before. (An indoor track is only 200 meters, so she had to run three times around to complete the race.) During the second lap, Heather moved into first place, looking strong and confident coming into the third and final lap. This is when it all changed for Heather, the leader of the pack. With one lap to go, her foot was tapped from behind. She lost her balance, tripped, and went straight down to the ground. The crowd gasped. The initial expectation was that Heather would just roll off the track and accept her unfortunate circumstance.

In an incredible display of all–out will, Heather jumped back up and started running again. At this point in the race, the other competitors were out ahead of her by 30 meters with only 200 meters left in the race. In one of the most amazing comebacks I've ever witnessed, Heather pushed forward overtaking each competitor until there was only one left. At this point, I, as a viewer, was on my feet shouting, "Come on! Come on! You can do it!" Incredibly, within the last 20 meters, Heather ran down the final runner and lunged forward for the victory! Every time I watch the video, I'm overcome by the human potential we ALL share when we simply refuse to give up.

God has given me breath to run in this race called life, and, unfortunately, I face–planted…hard. I hurt others with my actions, and I temporarily separated myself from the One who loves me beyond my comprehension. When I was faced with the very lowest moments of my existence, there on the hard ground of failure, I was presented with a choice. In that moment, I wasn't aware of what a decision in either direction would entail for my life and family, but Jesus did. Through the power of the Holy Spirit, I faintly heard His kind and loving voice say, "Come on! Come on! You can do it!"

I understand with deep compassion and empathy how difficult it is to rise, even to your knees, when you are down, especially when you're covered with what feels like a hundred pound blanket of shame, but you can rise, my friend, you can rise. How do I know? I know because it is the will of God for all of us who call on Him to thrive in Him. No matter what you feel in the present tense about your life, this is the truth. He wouldn't call us His children if it weren't so.

Yet to all who did receive him, to those who believed in his name, he gave the right to become children of God.
John 1:12

I also understand the conflict from wanting this passionately, but not knowing how to get there. I perceive how a wounded perspective about the parent/child relationship can cloud your judgment. I know how difficult and heartbreaking it can be to exist in that place of confusion, shame, and doubt, but I'll reiterate: you can rise out of that hole of despair.

The answer is found in the verbs—words that have action associated with them. Words like: ask, believe, acknowledge, receive, repent, forgive, communicate, surrender, give, and the list goes on. If you are having a difficult time thinking of yourself in relation to your Heavenly Father with these action words, then it is time to make a choice. The Author of your story is waiting to help you up and reclaim those specific pages of your life that have been damaged or torn. He is good and trustworthy, faithful and kind. Our Father is willing and able, awesome and holy. Please take it from one who has tasted life free of bondage and isolation…IT IS GOOD!

Finishing strong should not only be a personal goal, but should also emanate from us as our greatest honor in touching, guiding, and releasing the next generation. If you are a parent, this begins with your children, your most precious gifts endowed to you by the Lord. They are really what's at stake when you choose what might seem like the easy path that ultimately leads to death, in lieu of the hard, narrow path that leads to life.

Enter through the narrow gate. For wide is the gate and broad is the road that leads to destruction, and many enter through it. But small is the gate and narrow the road that leads to life, and only a few find it.
Matthew 7:13–14

This passage is true for salvation, but also for every decision henceforth that has the potential for a ripple effect in our lives and in the lives of those we love. We just don't live on this planet for ourselves, and once we've been given the chance to lead those who are counting on us, it is imperative we take it seriously. I know I didn't initially understand the impact my private choices would have on my children until it was almost too late. I was so warped by my woundedness that I had difficulty putting things together because it was so painful.

For those who ask me now, I gladly speak of the pain and of the intense process my wife and I have affectionately termed "the backhoe of our lives." Essentially, no stone was left unturned and every unhealthy root was dug up and cleared away. Painful? You bet. Worth it? Absolutely! You may be thinking, "What does that have to do with the next generation?" It has everything to do with our children and their children and so on because it is our legacy we pass down to them—both spiritually and emotionally.

This includes what is in the light, as well as what is locked in darkness behind a closed door. If you want to finish strong, I have learned that it is impossible in eternal terms to do so unless you're living openly and honestly, first with the Lord and then with others. That is why Jesus was right there with me when I was facedown on the mat and the enemy started the ten count smiling and salivating because he thought he had won. *1, 2, 3.* "Come on! Come on! You can do it!" Jesus said to me. *4, 5, 6.* Again my Lord whispered, "Come on! You know my voice." *7, 8, 9.* "Beloved, my lambs are at stake!" You see, the enemy of my soul knew that if he took me out, he would take out numerous lives with one fell swoop. That is why he works so hard to mar the image of God by dismantling marriages and families with secrecy, lust, isolation, and shame. Thousands upon thousands are being lulled to sleep, thinking they can take their baggage with them to their grave and it won't have any lasting effects on the ones they love. My friend, that's not the case, and that's not finishing strong. Please know that I say these words not in condemnation, but with great humility and passion for "I was blind, but now I see" (*Amazing Grace*).

It is our best contribution while residing on this earth to live out the words of Proverbs 22:6 (NKJV).

Train up a child in the way he should go, and when he is old he will not depart from it.

Translated from the Hebrew, this passage literally means, "Initiate a child in accordance with his way."[5] This means that not only am I responsible for instructing my child in the ways of the Lord, but I am also charged with hearing the Holy Spirit regarding his or her gifts, future calling, and their "niche," if you will. This is very important, because to help guide a child in their gifting, you must be present and accounted for as a parent, physically, spiritually, and emotionally. This is difficult if you are spending a good portion of your time and energy nursing an ongoing wound, living in populated isolation, or partaking of a secret sin.

During our family restoration, Teri and I came to terms with this proverbial mandate in a new and profound way. It was one of the most empowering exercises for us to really hear the Lord speak directly into our lives with what Dr. Ted called our "prophetic promises." These prophetic promises are our individual "Godprints," or in other words, who we are and what we are called to do by our Creator.

It was equally empowering as parents to go through the same process with and on behalf of our daughters. Don't be misled to believe that once we prayed and heard the Lord for ourselves and our girls that our involvement ended, rather it was just the beginning. We are now charged with covering, guiding, challenging, and, most importantly, protecting that which the Lord placed in them when He created them.

The enemy targets with laser–point accuracy the area in which we are most gifted and called by the Lord. I saw it in my own life with the wounding he inflicted on my sensitive heart, a heart that was meant to feel deeply for others, not build walls and

---

5 Bible Hub, "Pulpit Commentary" http://biblehub.com/commentaries/pulpit/proverbs/22.htm (accessed Mar. 19, 2015).

form compartments. We were given revelation into the lifelong attack on Teri's calling by silencing her voice and diminishing her confidence, both of which she now walks in freely. So, when Teri and I see our daughters moving and operating "in accordance with their way," we see the handiwork of God in our midst. We are relentless in being present spiritually, physically, and emotionally in their lives by encouraging them in these ways. When necessary, we stand in the gap between the enemy's destructive plan against their future callings and their precious hearts. It's our mandate, but it is also our joy, our purpose, and our most precious legacy.

PARTING WORDS...

I was reluctant to write the words in this book because it is such a fragile and controversial issue, and I wrestled with it being attached to me out there in the wide world of criticism and judgment. But, that reluctance was just fear rearing its ugly head again in my life. It's a new language I speak with my Father and my loved ones, a language of honesty and vulnerability. From one who has come out of captivity and bondage into a place of freedom and peace, a split second in that old place is far too long and much too costly. This story, as hard as it was for everyone involved, must be told because too many people are still in captivity and willing to stay there, not understanding that there is a way out.

If you were sitting right across from me and we were having this discussion, you would see the intensity and compassion in my eyes when I say, "Please don't stay there, my friend." You and your loved ones are worth more than that. Jesus demonstrated that by hanging on a cross for you and me, and every moment of our lives that we accept the captivity—mentality, spiritually, or physically—is an affront to His indescribable love.

You may remember at the beginning of my story I mentioned that God had to do a double-sided exposure in my life. With righteous judgment He exposed the sin that caused so much damage, but with inexplicable gentleness, He also exposed the lies I had believed in my heart about Him and myself, His creation. You may relate to the young child named Jamie who had his sensitive heart wounded by unfortunate life circumstances. You may feel like the leper who longs for a touch that will forever change your life. You may identify with the term "populated isolation" and have come to a place in your life where being alone is all you believe you are capable of. It may have hit home when you read of the not-so-great-wizard whose persona is uncovered when the curtain is pulled away, exposing just a man pushing buttons and pulling levers, trying to hold it all together. It may have touched your heart to think of the possibility that Jesus would step between you and your accuser and call you His own, and you may be reading this feeling exhausted and at the end of your rope, desperately hoping there is more than the crazy pace you are running in a futile attempt to feel loved and accepted.

You see, exposure is not a bad thing when it's done under the right light. When you have been fumbling around in darkness and deception in one way or another for too long, you don't even know what the right kind of light is capable of anymore. It's like using a dim and flickering flashlight to find out if you have a deadly internal disease when you have at your disposal a high-powered CT Scanner.

Jesus spoke to the people once more and said, "I am the light of the world. If you follow me, you won't have to walk in darkness, because you will have the light that leads to life."
John 8:12 (NLT)

What kind of life is Jesus referring to in this passage? I can attest that it is beyond description in earthly terms because it is an echo of our eternity in Heaven. That is why I am writing these words, friend, because we were all made for more than what this earth has to offer. It's time to wake up to the sobering reality that the issue of pornography isn't going away unless we all choose the right thing, which is most often the hardest thing. It is not only about the struggling soul, but also about the believers in our world taking ownership for ourselves and providing a place for healing and change. Do you know what brings Teri and me to tears these days? The thought that well over half of our nation is in bondage associated with pornography and very few seem to even care. The next generation has very little chance of eradicating this present danger if those who go before them are either teaching addictive patterning or are too busy to notice. Marriages and families are ripping apart, precious people are being exploited, and some very unsavory characters are making billions of dollars a year, all while the church seems unwilling, or maybe even afraid, to stand up and face this head on. I am not standing in judgment by saying this, for I was unwilling and ill–equipped to deal with it myself, because I was a slave to it. I've spoken with too many leaders who are speaking the language of denial, repression, and hopelessness, and it breaks my heart. There is nothing like being saved and set free, and my heart is full of empathy for those still trapped in the lethal cycle of addiction.

In Romans 12:1–2 Paul speaks of being transformed.

Therefore, I urge you, brothers and sisters, in view of God's
mercy, to offer your bodies as a living sacrifice, holy and
pleasing to God—this is your true and proper worship.
Do not conform to the pattern of this world,
but be transformed by the renewing of your mind.
Then you will be able to test and approve what God's will is—
his good, pleasing and perfect will.

I started my life journey as a wounded boy, and from the ashes Jesus refined a broken man into a disciple. That is my highest calling. Finishing strong is about transforming into God's intended best for us as individuals. But, it involves an offering— ourselves and an altar. I pray earnestly that what we are offering people who are being drawn by the Holy Spirit to lay down their struggles is in fact an altar, and not the back door. I understand this process is messy, it's controversial, and it's rarely easy, but it involves the precious people Jesus died for. The beauty of this transformative process is that it postures us perfectly to be His instruments in this world to contribute to another person's transformative process. It's discipleship and multiplication in its purest form. This is where things are breaking down, my friend.

If the current statistics are anywhere near valid, then the beauty of discipleship is being marred and damaged under the weight of sin and brokenness. It seems these days that the term "discipleship" has become one of those overused words. Call it what you will, but an intentional, biblically focused, long–suffering, Spirit–led, and sacrificial process with trusted individuals is what it takes to finish strong. Are we willing? We must be willing, no matter what Pandora's Box you or anyone you know may be afraid to open. Jesus didn't mince words when He said, "Therefore, go into all the world and make disciples" (Matthew 28:19). He knew it was this sacred and steadfast exchange that would change the world. The principle still applies. The world awaits.

WORDS OF GRATITUDE & JOY

Dear Teri, Rachel, Elise, and Grace,

I write this letter with a heart full of gratitude and joy. I am the wealthiest man on this earth because God has blessed me with all of you! In this letter I want to share with you how I see you now, through the new lens of health that my Father in Heaven has given me. I have always loved all four of you, but in my brokenness I didn't love you the way God intended. I now see so clearly and beautifully the inexpressible value of each of you in the sight of God's pure light. You all have been so patient and loving toward me as I have walked out this journey of healing. You have cheered me on when I became frustrated and discouraged with myself. You stood by me as I left the old me behind, and became the upgraded version that God first intended me to be. These words in this letter come from my heart. As I draw closer to my Father in Heaven and become the husband and father that you deserve here on earth, my joy increases exponentially!

Teri, you are the love of my life. There is no one on earth that I desire to be with more than you. We have walked through so many valleys and stood on numerous mountaintops together, but nothing compares to the path that we now walk on. You have been the purest example of God's grace and love that I have ever seen or experienced before in my life. You have been faithful in your love and commitment to me, even when the back door was open wide. When God brought us together on July 11, 1992, He was happy and I was happy! Through the challenges that this life has brought our way, you have walked through each one keeping your eyes on your Loving Father in Heaven, never giving up and never turning back. You have allowed God to form and shape you into the perfect and precious jewel that you are and it gives me great joy to watch as the world is now being able to see and experience what I have had the privilege to witness. I consider it the greatest honor to stand by your side, love you with the love of Christ, cover you in prayer, be your number one cheerleader, and press through on the journey called life hand in hand. I wake up each day thanking God for you and the opportunity to be your armor bearer as you press forward, fulfilling your God–given destiny and our destiny together in unity. I love you with all that I am, and with everything in me. I am excited to grow old with you, the one I love.

Rachel, I am so proud of you. You are a young women who reflects the compassion and love of Jesus to the world around you. Your gentle confidence shines in a world that is dark and hopeless. The love that has developed in your life illuminates your surroundings like a lighthouse on top of the world. I consider it a privilege and honor to stand by your side as you navigate the journey that God has before you. I have watched you cling to your Heavenly Father in your darkest hours. I have seen you love, even when you felt unloved. I have watched you extend hands of grace to those who are longing to be loved and accepted. You are a beautiful young woman of God, and I am so thankful that I get to be your daddy, and the man who will stand and support you throughout your life.

Elise, you might be small, but you are mighty! Your convictions are steadfast and will not be shaken. I stand and watch you struggle with the injustice of this world, and declare that you will not partake, nor become what you have seen. You have deposited the Word of God deep down in your heart, which has become the rudder to your soul. God has placed you in the middle of the arena of life to lead your generation to truth. You don't mind being out front, and I can see in you a deep responsibility to stay the course on which God has placed you. I will always be right by your side as you contend for all that God has for your generation and generations to come.

Grace, you are our Mother Teresa. Your love and compassion will turn many to the heart of the Father. Your kindness and merciful heart will be your greatest weapon wielded against the enemy, and many will receive healing for their soul from the gift that God has placed in you. You have a heart of innocence that permeates the environment around you. You have a great calling here on earth, but in your heart you are ready for the journey ahead. I will always be by your side as long as I am here on earth. I burst with excitement for the journey God has planned for you. You will always be my little Gracie with your precious little hand pressing against my face saying, "I love you, Daddy."

My dearest girls, I am committed to all of you as the Craft family now moves forward in health. By His great love, God has exposed the true Craft family, and now we can live and thrive with confidence in the purpose that has been placed on our lives. I am excited for the new memories that await us as we live each day together.

Your devoted husband and father,
James

ENDORSEMENTS

Exposed is a beautiful example of faith, hope, strength, and honest transparency. I will forever admire how Teri's deep love for the Lord has given wings to a comeback story few ever witness in their lifetime. Her account of the struggles and relentless fight for her marriage and for her family is simply inspiring. A must read!

CHERYL MOANA MARIE SABATO
Songwriter & Artist Management

It's apparent when reading through *Exposed* that it is a truly transparent and honest outpouring from James & Teri's personal experience. It speaks deeply of God's never-ending love and grace. We applaud their willingness to share their darkest moments, with a sincere and genuine purpose of encouraging the reader through the words of their testimony. (Revelation 12:11)

DAVID & GINA HANLEY
Founders & President of Dream Label Group

James and Teri Craft are brave. Their timely book, *Exposed*, presents essential life lessons for each of us in a binocular view with both Teri and James disclosing the same account, yet with divergent compasses. Theirs is a story that illustrates the old adage: *You will either be ruled by the rudder or ruled by the rocks*. One was an expedition that led to repentance and the other a courageous passage that led to forgiveness. They have navigated their past, but are not moored there. Rather, they have boldly chosen to set sail towards a bright future, for that is where the promises of God await.

DR. WAYNE CORDEIRO
Pastor & Author

I am so grateful for the courage and honesty of James and Teri Craft. They have penned a page–turner that makes way for freedom and healing, while sharing about a subject matter that needs to be brought to light more. *Exposed* unveils more than their story, which is powerful, it exposes our constant need for Jesus in every inch of our walk.

TIFFANY THURSTON
Worship Leader & Founder of the BLOOM Conference

The journey through betrayal can be one of the most excruciating experiences a wife never imagines she will ever have to face. I watched, at close range, how Teri made decision after decision to trust God with all the heart–wrenching emotions she experienced, as she chose to walk through the healing process. In Teri's story, you will see how God gave her insight and revelation through His Word and His Spirit to not only process her pain and work through forgiveness, but to also believe for and reach out to new beginnings. I am so proud of both Teri and James and the heroic steps they both took to embrace deeper levels of intimacy in their relationship with God and with each other.

DIANE ROBERTS
Co–Founder of Pure Desire Ministries International
Author of *Betrayal & Beyond: Healing for Broken Trust*

EXPOSED
A JOURNEY OF RENEWAL & HOPE

JAMES & TERI CRAFT

EXPOSED
A JOURNEY OF RENEWAL & HOPE
by James & Teri Craft

© 2015 by James & Teri Craft and Pure Desire Ministries International

ALL RIGHTS RESERVED

Published by:
Pure Desire Ministries International
www.puredesire.org | Gresham, Oregon | March 2015

ISBN: 978–0–9896598–5–7

TERI'S STORY **TABLE OF CONTENTS**

*Exposed…*there could not have been a better title chosen for this story. This word describes the many places that have been laid bare in the journey the Crafts have taken. It has been painful and joyful to walk with them through it. Having known Teri and James for more than a decade prior to this, it wasn't until the exposure began that I could see how their marriage and ministry was enmeshed. Once I began to see the real Teri and James, it was all too familiar; I had lived this way myself for thirty–two years until an emotional crash happened in my life that awakened me to grace and health. This type of enmeshment is the entanglement and entrapment of lives without boundaries, souls without identities apart from their "doing," and marriages that are unhealthily intertwined with leadership roles in ministry. One of the greatest places of derailment for pastors is when there is no differentiation between their ministry life and their personal life, when husband and wife are more co–pastors than co–heirs together of the grace of life.

Now, though I fully understand the assignment the Lord has given me, it does not define me. Whether my husband and I serve in ministry together, or not, we are first and foremost husband and wife, life partners who find the joy in our intimacy based on our interdependence rather than co–dependence. Our commitment of love is to the person, first and foremost, not the pastor–leader. Our friendships are not dependent upon the titles we, or our friends, have. We stand by and "speak the truth in love" to our friends, not shrinking back because of our role. Our ministry assignments have responsibilities that we joyfully accept, as well as the responsibility for the wake we leave from our leadership decisions. However, jobs, churches, and colleagues will come and go throughout our lifetime, so we must differentiate between our relationships and our roles. I once heard, if you put your hand into a five-gallon bucket of water and then quickly pull it out, the amount of time it takes for the water to fill back in is how long people remember you after you have been replaced. Though strong language, there is truth in the meaning.

Having walked through the recovery and now the lifelong restoration process with my friends, Teri and James Craft, I have observed a couple who is discovering these truths I've written about and are falling in love with each other in a new and profound way. I am watching two individuals committed to growth in personal health. While it is not the way one wants to learn these transformative life lessons, they have submitted their hearts and behaviors to their Father, their church, and friends who have come alongside them, and are now turning exposure into a lifestyle. Teri and James are living open and honest lives with everything exposed to their God and one another so that light shines on every aspect, where no darkness or even a shadow is allowed to stay. They have taken this one step further—they have chosen to share their story in an extremely vulnerable, transparent manner…on written pages for everyone to read, knowing there is a risk in being exposed. Yet, if their pain and healing can help you see your own area of need and see that true health and restoration is possible, maybe, just maybe, you will see that living *Exposed* is the greatest freedom any human being can experience.

Considering myself (Galatians 6:1),
Tammy Dunahoo
Friend of the Craft Family

ACKNOWLEDGMENTS

Love is not love
Which alters when it alteration finds,
Or bends with the remover to remove:
O no! it is an ever-fixed mark
That looks on tempests and is never shaken....
William Shakespeare

To my Jesus, thank you for being the ever-fixed mark of love that carried me through this journey.

To James, you are my forever love. Thank you for not giving up on yourself and for being open to the discovery of what is really true love. Thank you for being you.

To Rachel, Elise, and Grace, I will forever be changed by your pure love and strength. It is my deepest joy to see you bloom into the rare and unique individuals that you were created to be by your Heavenly Father. You are strong. You are beautiful. You are loved.

To the beautiful people of Hawaii, New Hope Oahu, and Foursquare Hawaii District, and to Pastor Wayne and Anna Cordeiro, who all extended the hand of "Ohana" when we needed it the most, **Mahalo, Mahalo Nui Loa.**

INTRODUCTION

On April 25, 2013, my life changed forever. The day began like any other, with an early morning alarm followed by a pushed rush to get our three beautiful girls ready for school. It was the tune we'd rehearsed to perfection. A brief chat with my husband about the upcoming day of ministry, schedule interchanges, and a family prayer were always on order. As I bustled through my pleasant reality, I had no idea this was its last morning.

The following pages are a memoir of sorts, a glimpse into my "aha" moments, and an honest, heartfelt plea to you, dear reader, to carefully consider the fragile nature of our lives. The touch and smell of tragedy is something I know firsthand, but I also know firsthand the faithfulness of our Father. I hope to share with you how He covered me in my greatest time of need and how He spoke gentle words of encouragement and direction that opened my heart to a love story I never knew could exist.

I offer you my perspective on the church experience as a previous insider—turned reluctant outsider—which may, if your heart is open, prove helpful when you attempt to minister to the broken and hurting brother or sister sitting right beside you on Sunday morning.

In this process of discovery and restoration, I uncovered a mammoth-sized issue and the gaping hole it is leaving in our society today. It is quietly dismantling churches and families from the inside out. As the Christian community, we are essentially breeding an addicted and broken generation in our slowness to come to terms with the fact that many of us are living broken and addicted lives ourselves. A few years ago, I would have read that statement and thought it was just a biased opinion and, frankly, too uncomfortable of a subject to pay much attention to…until addiction came to my doorstep and robbed our family of almost everything.

It is important for every believer to grasp the reality of this present danger, not as one who sits on the periphery, but as one who recognizes the danger in each of our own lives, families, and churches. There are too many good people hemorrhaging from the pain of addiction and feeling they have no place to go. Subsequent to this is the reality that there are also many innocent people bearing the scars of the devastation produced by this deadly web. Please don't misunderstand my heart when I say that judgment and shame have not only caused a great deal of the issue, but are keen in the perpetuation of it. When judgment comes largely from the evangelical portion of our society upon its own, it is heartbreaking.

Offering help that makes a difference is not about casting judgment or simply telling people "no" or "don't do that again." It's about investing in people and finding out what's really going on in the hearts and minds of these people for whom the Father loves and Jesus died. It's more about discovering who we are in Christ, realizing the startling truth that many of us have baggage and abusive patterning we've been carrying since we were children, and honestly coming to terms with how we've learned to medicate that pain. When, statistically ,sixty to seventy percent of adult men and twenty to thirty percent of adult women struggle to the point of addiction with pornography,[1] the ripple effect of what that does to erode a person's life and all of their relationships should leave us breathless. When we are seeing the most addicted generations to date walk this earth, truly more than just the simple shake of the head in disgust is needed.

The prescription for this situation is first and foremost true knowledge about addictive patterning and sexual addiction, and then a firm commitment of the church to rise up and stop ignoring the issue that is consuming and destroying the lives of more than half of our congregations and communities…period. I'm talking about hundreds of thousands of precious people like you and me, not just numbers on a page or lifeless statistics, that are being harmed on a daily basis through a vicious addictive cycle. My prayer is that this book will begin to stir in your spirit something that looks like change, motivated by courageous love.

My story is a beautiful and pure representation of the grace God extends to the hearts of those He calls His own. I will never be the same. One cannot stand in nakedness before the Lord as I have, stripped of all I thought identified me, embraced by the Father in the most hidden places of my soul, and not be utterly transformed. I've come to love my husband more than I ever thought possible, and considering the potentially devastating outcomes that could have resulted from the betrayal and pain of his actions, it is again another beautiful example of what love and forgiveness in Christ can accomplish. He is more courageous than anyone I know, and I am proud to call him my forever love.

We are taking back, one hard–fought day at a time, what the enemy has been attempting to steal from us ever since we were little children. We are breaking the generational bondage that

---

1   Jeremy & Tiana Wiles, *Conquer Series: The Battle Plan for Purity*, DVD 1 (West Palm Beach, FL: Kingdomworks Studios, 2013) conquerseries.com.

would have been passed on if it weren't for the power of the Holy Spirit and our fierce commitment to change the patterns of our behavior.

For those looking for a fresh version of reality entertainment, I encourage you to look elsewhere, because this exposition is a testimony of the love our Father wraps around the broken–hearted and the forgiveness found in no other place, but at the foot of the cross. I argued with the Lord about writing this memoir. I'm still in the process of working through many of the things stated within it. I believe I heard the Lord say to my heart, simply this, "Will you be brave enough, my child, to paddle over and share your life raft with another who feels the same way you do right now?"

He reminded me of the many times I cried in my car or curled up in a ball on my bedroom floor and wailed, grieving the loss of my former life, and waiting for friends to call who just plain didn't call. You see, my story makes people uncomfortable. Very few want to touch the unseemly reality of a pastor human enough to fail. And so they stay away.

The betrayal hits from all sides in a story like ours, and it feels almost unbearable. Horrific pain comes to every family member, first at home, and then as they bear rejection from other Christians. The agony I felt knowing that my obliterated former life was beyond my ability to fix was acute. Oh, how alone I was, as if I'd survived the sinking of the Titanic and was now floating in the icy waters of the Atlantic Ocean. But my Father's call resonated in my heart, "Will you be brave enough, my child, to paddle over and share your life raft with another who feels the same way you do right now? Will you be courageous enough to honestly speak of your journey, so someone else will hear of My hope in the midst of their pain? Will you be willing to be transparent, to admit that the way is difficult to navigate, when the map is still being explored and drafted? Will you risk further rejection, so that even one might find the path to freedom?" I've answered His questions to me and I've written my story for you, dear reader.

Essentially, I'm asking you to put on your hiking boots and take this journey with me. In the upcoming chapters, you will read my story. On the flip side of this book, you can read my husband's story. I pray you will be open to journeying with him, as well. Together, in our individual perspectives, we will give you a glimpse of the fragility of the human condition and the power of our Lord and Savior to heal and restore…no matter who you are, what title you possess, or what you've uncovered in the dark of night.

To all those whose lives are turned upside down, and to those who feel alone…

For the heart afraid to risk losing it all in order to do the right thing…

To the dear soul in need of hope, and to anyone who cares enough to help those who are suffering…

These words are for you.
Don't be afraid.

Chapter 1
TICK TOCK

Pursue, and all will be recovered.

The Life Journal reading for the day was 1 Samuel 30. I vividly remember the impact it had on me. It was one of those quiet moments with the Lord and His Word that changes you from the inside out, and you know it. I had no idea the kind of preparation Jesus was doing in me until I looked back in hindsight. He was gearing me up for the battle of my life. I didn't recognize it at the time, but I have been overwhelmingly grateful to Him every day since. This was my journal entry for the day:

APRIL 25, 2013
"STAY THE COURSE" 1 SAMUEL 30:6–8

Scripture: *Now David was greatly distressed, for the people spoke of stoning him, because the soul of all the people was grieved, every man for his sons and his daughters. But David strengthened himself in the Lord his God[…] So David inquired of the Lord, saying, "Shall I pursue this troop? Shall I overtake them?" And He answered him, "Pursue, for you shall surely overtake them and without fail recover all."*

Observation: *Even though David was grieved and distressed because his family and everything he owned was taken away, he looked to the Lord. He didn't let adversity stop him from seeking the Lord. Due to his right heart and obedience, the Lord rewards David with victory, not only for his family, but also for all those who followed him.*

Application: *As a leader in ministry and as a wife and parent, it's so important to have an undying focus for the Lord and His will. When the enemy comes to kill, steal, and destroy, it is then that I must forcibly take my focus off the situation and put it back on the Lord.*

Prayer: *Jesus, help me seek You in every situation. I pray for a heart after Yours. When I am tempted to move away from You or Your will, I pray Your Holy Spirit will bring me back to You.*

It's crazy how God puts things together. The journal entry that morning evoked thoughts of an encounter with the Lord that was equally impactful just one week prior. I was sitting at my daughter's diving practice at the University of Hawaii, where she enjoyed the training of a great junior diving program. The two-hour practice afforded me ample reading time in the warm tropical sun. I had grabbed a little book that someone had given me a few years back, but I had never read, called *For Women Only* by Shaunti Feldhahn. The catchy title got my attention that morning, so I tucked it into my purse and we headed to the pool.

What a great read! As I flipped through the pages, I was surprised by what I found. The entire book gives information for women about how we can understand more fully the thoughts, challenges, and motivations of men. In my mind, I heard myself thinking, *Do men really feel that insecure at times? Do they really struggle with feelings of inadequacy to the degree the statistics are stating?*

It was as if the author had given me a glimpse into a part of my husband I had never considered. He always seemed so confident and in charge. Could he be feeling as if he doesn't measure up? *Hello…where have I been?* I thought. It was a revelation. I simply hadn't thought about this before.

I began to press in and pray specifically for James in the areas that were listed as struggles for men. It opened up my heart toward my husband in ways I had never before imagined. During that week after reading the book, the Lord spoke gently to my heart, "You are his armor bearer." This was appealing to me at the time, because my mind immediately went to the grandiose thought that it meant we were to see an incredible increase in our effectiveness in ministry and influence. Naturally, I thought God was calling me to come alongside James as he stepped into new and exciting places for the Lord.

As I did some further study that week, I was struck with the account of Jonathan and his relationship with his armor bearer in 1 Samuel 14. What set them apart in their relationship was that they were essentially of one mind, or together, "heart and soul." *Cool,* I thought, *James and I will be of one mind when we take the world for Jesus. After all, this is what we had been doing our entire married life in one way or another, right?* We started as volunteer youth sponsors in college and transitioned to youth pastors as a young family, leading multiple overseas mission trips. Then, James stepped into greater roles in speaking and leading for the next generation, as our denomination's national youth director. This phase of our lives culminated with us as senior pastors. James' current position was lead campus pastor at New Hope Oahu, an amazing church with global influence in Hawaii.

As I finished writing my journal entry one week later on April 25th, I couldn't help feeling as if those very words were directly for James and me in some way. It seemed the Lord had imparted a special something to me in our time together, and it was powerful, but I wasn't sure exactly what was transpiring. The verse played in my mind again, "Pursue, for you shall surely overtake them and without fail recover all." Pursue what? I kept thinking. Again, I rehearsed our familiar "go to," which was ministry. This must have a ministry application.

I know now that the words were an encouragement for our very lives, marriage, and family; my initial application was slightly off. I had no idea what was coming our way, nor the reality of what I would come to understand firsthand. I did not know that I would soon stand face-to-face with betrayal, loss, tragedy, and addiction, but He did. My Daddy God knew that driving down the Kalanianaole Hwy, heading straight for me, was my husband of twenty years, bringing with him the truth that would change my world in a split second.

I remember distinctly where I was when James surprised me in the late morning on that April day. I can even hear the doves cooing outside our bedroom window and the smell of plumeria that pervaded our little townhome. He came into the bedroom crying uncontrollably. I gripped the door jam and braced myself for something big.

"Is something wrong with the girls?" I gasped. He shook his head no. "Did something happen with our family? Is my Mom okay?" He shook his head in response. By this time he was kneeling on the floor and my breath had been stolen from my lungs.

"I was unfaithful to you back in California before we moved to Hawaii."

Slow motion. Sounds vanished. My heart stopped. All I remember was grabbing my keys and running full speed down the road that led out of our quiet gated community called Kuapa Isle, and onto Hawaii Kai Drive toward our two youngest girls' school, Ha'haione.

The crazy thing is that I remember each step as if it were yesterday. I was devastated beyond words, like my heart had been squeezed between two arms of a vice and burst right down the middle. I knew his words meant everything had changed. My heart had been broken and betrayed; my marriage was probably over, and it was inevitable that our family would suffer the consequences of his actions in more ways than I could fathom, starting with the fact that we would be immediately asked to step down in ministry.

I had been serving in ministry enough years to know what the next steps looked like, and it was the scariest place I have ever been in in my entire life. My worst nightmare had come to life and was chasing me down the road, but I couldn't outrun it.

Strangely, I also experienced a very keen sense of something that felt like relief, as if the lid of the pressure cooker of our lives had finally been lifted off and all the steam and fog had dissipated. It didn't make any cognitive sense at the time, but through intense discovery and recovery that still lay ahead, I came to understand how my heart and spirit could have been displaying such divergent emotions all at the same moment in time.

I was a wife who had been taken through a vicious cycle for years and never really understood the cause. Anger, isolation, and manipulation, mingled with beautiful kindness, love, and caring was my world—a pressure cooker indeed.

I must have been a sight, running full speed down the road with no shoes on my feet, looking like I was escaping from death itself. All I kept saying over and over was, "Jesus help me," and "Where do I go from here?"

Then, suddenly, I experienced something that is difficult to express in words. The most unexplainable and unimaginable presence I have ever felt in my life consumed me. It was like a warm blanket and a rushing wind all at the same time. It was my Lord and Savior; I had felt His touch before, but this time it was exponential. He uttered these words in the sweetest voice I had ever heard, straight into the deepest part of my soul:

"Pursue, and all will be recovered."

I stopped because I literally couldn't take another step. I grabbed my weak knees for support and breathed in and out, in and out: those long, deep breaths that fill your lungs with life–giving oxygen. "What?" I said, as I began to weep. I knew it was my Jesus. He was present, running with me in my darkest moment. He was there. This was *rhema*: God's revealed word to me. His utterance circumvented my situation and frantic state by placing His love letter directly into my heart by way of His Spirit.

"Armor bearer," is what I heard next. It was like my Savior was whispering in my ear all the words of preparation He had planted in my heart the week leading up to this moment; He knew I would need them. Our lives and our future depended on them.

I felt my body and emotions calm down in what I can only describe as peace and hope amidst the devastation that lay before me. I'd never before been able to describe in words what hope meant to me until this moment in time. Sure, I could quote Bible verses and give descriptive definitions, but I can say with all honesty, it was like the Lord gave me an infusion of hope as with an IV right into my veins. It wasn't the application we normally find ourselves in when we use this word, like, "I hope I get a parking spot in the crowded mall," or "I hope I get that job," or even, "I hope my prayer gets answered." This was the kind of hope that compels you to take your next breath when you feel as if you are done for—the hope found in Jesus— when all other earthly hopes have failed you and you lift your countenance upward and know you're not alone. I didn't know all of what the Holy Spirit was making clear to me, but I had been walking with the Lord long enough to know when He is speaking to my heart, and this encounter was extraordinary.

I turned my body around in that instant and began to walk toward home, completely relying on the God in whom I had put my whole trust and life. "Pursue, and all will be recovered." I heard it again in my heart. But, this time it was like an echo, a beautiful reminder, a promise that I had believed for years, but never had the ability or insight to comprehend its longing. Longing…it's an appropriate term for my heart's yearning in relation to my life and marriage.

For years I had known something was off. It had always been a mystery to me when such terrible anger would erupt from this normally gentle and loving man. For years I had known James and I were in need of help, but our ministry positions, our fear and pride, my inability to let anyone close enough to really know me, and his inability to let anyone really know him, put us on a crash course, and it was only a matter of time. Time, it seemed, had caught up with us, and it was relentless. The life I knew was now gone.

I say this cautiously, not wanting any reader to get the notion that I ever thought in a million years that this would have happened to us, but when it did, I realized deep down that there was not only shock and sadness from the betrayal, but also a feeling of regret. Why hadn't I sensed this? Why hadn't I done something earlier to prevent this? All I could do was take one step at a time toward home and believe my Heavenly Father would be my guide.

CHAPTER 1 – TICK TOCK

The next few days were filled with activities that you would expect from a wife whose husband had just passed away. I called family and friends and informed them of our situation, made parting plans with our dear church and pastor, talked to denominational leaders, procured a moving company to bring our belongings and cars back to the mainland, and helped our girls finish the school year, all while being an ocean away from our family in California.

It was in these first few days that James opened up to the fact that he had a real problem, one that had been there in one form or another ever since he was a little boy. He couldn't express exactly all of the details of why it had been there since his early childhood years, just that he was a very shameful and worthless individual, and had felt like that for most of his life. One morning, as we sat on our lanai that overlooked the dock and waterway connected to our townhome, he admitted to me, "I've tried to run so long from my pain that I eventually became dependent on workaholism and pornography to help me escape. I think I have a real problem; I think I'm addicted and I need help to stop this madness." I'm sure there are many things that race through a person's brain when someone says they are addicted to something. For me, it was just a lot more confusion piled on top of the hurt and confusion I had already suffered. It was apparent to me that he was in a place that made him unable to make clear decisions for our family and I had to step in and take the lead. This is why the bulk of the communications and planning fell on me.

(You will read in depth about the intensity of the recovery from an addiction to pornography and what it entails later in this book, For now, it is helpful to interject that it is similar to coming off of cocaine.)

I had to look down the path before us that now included addiction recovery, along with marriage and family restoration, trust building, breaking generational bondages, and starting from scratch to build a new income–generating career. I have to pause for a moment and give God the glory right here and now, because as I am writing this, tears well up in my eyes. That is a ridiculous to–do list, and one I hope no one ever finds in front of them, but I can attest that God is able to do exceedingly abundantly above all we ask or think…for we are the living proof (Ephesians 3:20 NKJV).

THE COURAGE TO SET A NEW COURSE

I asked James to stay in our home, but to move downstairs until I could make sense of everything. I would lie awake every night in my bed alone. I hadn't slept alone for twenty years. It was surreal. I wanted so desperately for him to console me in my grief, but he was the cause. The arms that I depended on for most of my life to bring comfort were now kept at arm's length. I felt as if my covering and my confidant had been stolen away. Alone, wretchedly alone, is the only way to describe how I felt from the inside out. I had stopped eating, except for a few bites of food each day. I honestly couldn't eat, and believe me, for this half Italian woman, eating had never been a problem.

My saving grace came in the form of a friend, my Gina. What would I have done without her? She had been the one I called first with my tragic story and she would be the one who called me every day without fail for the first two months to "check in." I laugh now, as I think back, because she would ask me what I ate that day and if I was getting exercise. She reminded me that my girls needed a healthy mommy and that "God's got this, Teri, don't you forget it!" She understood my situation. She had seen God work a miracle in her life and marriage, and encouraged me that He was able to do the same for our family. She put aside her preconceived notions and personal reactions and just loved me. I began to understand true friendship through her expression of love to me. I had hundreds of acquaintances, but not many friends who knew me to my core. Many people responded to me in this tragic season, but few rolled up their sleeves and said, "I'm in this for the long haul."

It is a peculiar thing, because I received such loving messages from people all over the world at first. But then, when life got busy or they would come to grips with the anger they felt toward James' actions, they just stopped calling and texting. I had nothing to offer anyone anymore—no influential position, no seat of honor, no pastoral perspective. It was just me: broken-hearted, quirky me. I had to come to the sobering truth that God was showing me, through this difficult season, what a true friend looks like, that I had very few of this variety, and how I would eventually be healed enough to become one of those true friends.

I have been asked many times how I had the courage to choose to stay and walk this out with James. My response has been pretty much the same since that fateful April day. I had seen my Father's faithfulness displayed in my life numerous times before this tragedy, so I was able to trust that He sees my life laid out before Him. When He bids me go right or left, I have to believe it is He, not me, who can see the road that leads to life. I guess another way to say it is, I try my best to respond to His voice no matter the situation. If I start to choose in which situation I will listen to Him and which I think is just off limits, then I make His power in my life null and void.

The above answer usually gets a number of responses from people. I know there is a great deal of emotion and hurt in people who have experienced this kind of pain and adversity, and maybe for them things turned out differently. That can sometimes bring up feelings of anger and disappointment. I understand, and have no condemnation for anyone or any situation. I know that our life story represents the most fragile of human conditions, and inherently brings to the surface a great many feelings and responses from people. Please hear my heart when I say that if my loving and caring Father said for me to leave because of my safety, I would have gone. It wasn't codependency or fear that turned me around, it was the hand of my Father leading me. He was leading me to my destiny, and my destiny is to walk this journey with James. He knew, though my heart was broken, it was not beyond repair. He knew that though James had made hurtful choices, that wasn't who He had created him to be. Most of all, our Daddy God knew that we would both open our hearts to Him and lean into this recovery with all the strength and power we were offered in Him, thereby releasing His will for our lives. He knew, and He told us He knew—that was all we needed to get us through the hardest battle we had ever faced.

I look back at the words the Lord spoke to my heart in preparation for this journey and I've come to understand that "armor bearing" for us in marriage is more like a mutual occupation. We "armor bear" for each other. Not for gain, but for Christ–centered marital vitality, for our children, and to be a beautifully complete reflection of God displayed to this hopeless world. It has taken every ounce of strength and will to access the deep wounds that drove our decision–making processes and then let our loving Savior heal us of the damage WE BOTH carried. We both carried such deep wounds from our childhood that being of one mind was almost impossible. Then add to that sin, fear, addiction, and betrayal, and you get two ships passing in the night. The tragedy is that the solitary itinerary of our two cracked and compromised ships led to a destructive and devastating end. For James and me, that journey's end was really just the beginning—the beginning of a quest that would lead us to the ultimate discovery of who God had created us to be individually and as a married couple. We are each other's armor bearer, clad with the full armor of God. We are walking in health and battling against the enemy daily in unity of mind, body, and spirit. I pray for you and many others that our discovery will be a revelation of the possibilities of a willing heart in the hands of a Mighty God. The gripping truth is that we all, especially those of us in leadership, must make the decision to seek healing and wholeness our top priority, no matter what the cost. If not, the arrival of destruction is only a matter of time.

Chapter 2
NORTH SHORE EBENEZER

No one gets left behind or forgotten…

A little more than a week had passed on this new journey, and I felt as if I had survived a tsunami. All I had known and dreamed about for most of my married life was now effectively washed away. What remained were the ruins, what God had to work with to rebuild. It didn't seem like much; but, at the same time, it felt like everything.

I looked at my strong and courageous girls as I dropped them off at school. Their beautiful smiles and innocent eyes beamed back at me and I realized I was still the richest person alive. Though James was emotionally unstable and broken, he was now repentant and genuinely receptive to help and guidance offered to him to get healthy. *God, can you really put this back together?* I would think to myself on occasion. I needed the Lord in a way that was equivalent to needing air in my lungs. I would look to Him moment by moment, and in ways I had never accessed before in my busy and self–sustaining existence.

Our lives had come to a screeching halt. When you have more time than you know what to do with, it creates occasions to think, analyze, mull over. Then worry sets in, followed quickly by panic. To combat what feels like an inevitable progression, it takes a good portion of energy to focus on the Lord, His Word, and His promises to you. In other words, it's emotionally and physically exhausting.

It was also about this time that grief, sadness, and anger started to roll in like the consistent sets of waves we'd sit and watch as a family at our favorite surfing spot near our home in Hawaii Kai. In the early evenings before sunset, we'd watch intently as the swells formed out in the distance; in a few minutes, massive and powerful waves would crash against the rocks making even the solid ground beneath our feet shake. This was the experience I felt as the realization set in that this nightmare wasn't going away. I began to feel the shaking ground and it terrified me.

That was the day I called our denominational district supervisor, who was helping us with our next steps. He had offered us a little cottage on the North Shore that belonged to a very godly and generous man, if I ever felt we needed to just get away. As hard as it was to focus on the right thing instead of what I wanted to do individually, I believed I had peace in my heart that the change of scenery would do us all some good.

I spoke with Don, the homeowner, and made arrangements for our entire family to spend the weekend at his North Shore home. We packed our overnight bags, loaded up the car, and headed out of town. When we arrived, I instantly felt peace, as if I had come home. Out from the garage bounded a beautiful golden retriever named Koa, and our girls immediately fell in love. We were greeted by Don who helped us settle into the impeccably decorated cottage, built adjacent to the main house. Every need was taken into consideration when he constructed and stocked this cozy oasis for those in need of rest and recuperation.

I began to wonder about a person who would open their home to people like us, and how it seemed to speak of the loving kindness of my Heavenly Father in so many ways. I think it started to heal my heart before I even understood what was happening. We were then given the grand tour of the property. It's hard to express in words the view that opened up as we walked across the long grassy yard that led straight onto the picturesque North Shore beach. It was so stunningly beautiful that I forgot for a moment that my life was in shambles. I could see in our girls' faces that it was a special day and that this kindness would be remembered for years to come.

It was decided that everyone would rest a bit before hitting the beach, so James and the girls headed back to the cottage. I felt as if I needed just a little bit of time alone, so I walked along the shore for a while and settled on a quiet spot to sit and let the beauty of the surroundings calm my soul. I noticed in the distance that Koa was running back and forth on the beach, almost frantically looking for his master who had waded out a short distance past the surf for a swimming workout. It was a funny sight to watch this beautiful dog race side to side with every ounce of his attention and focus pointing outward toward the water. When he heard his master whistle, he stopped and repositioned himself, so that he was directly in alignment with him. Then another wave would come. Don would be farther down the beach, Koa would lose sight of him, and Koa would again go racing excitedly back and forth until he heard the familiar sound of his master's whistle. This went on awhile until Koa bolted straight out, braved the crashing waves, and joined his master in an afternoon swim beyond the breakers.

I commented to Don when he came in from his swim how I enjoyed watching Koa bound up and down the shore, desperate to keep his master in sight while he swam. He laughed a little and said that it was very uncharacteristic of Koa to do that. "He usually swims the whole time with me. That was unusual."

I sat there for a while with the trade winds brushing past my face and my toes and fingers curling in and out of the warm sand. I thought how often I feel like Koa on the beach. I think I lose sight of my Master—my Father—and I race around desperately trying to figure things out. I try to fix the situation in my own strength and timing, and I feel all alone in my efforts. It is when I brave the obstacles in front of me—not letting anything separate us—that I am at peace with His leading. It was the waves that kept Koa from seeing where his master was, not the great distance or his lack of effort. Likewise, it is my circumstances that often keep me from seeing Jesus when I need Him the most. Koa unknowingly ministered to my heart that day and was a great example for me that I should never let anything separate me from my Heavenly Father, not even big scary waves that shake the ground beneath my feet.

The evening was warm and the breeze was cool and sweet—smelling, like it had picked up the tropical flowers and salty surf and carried it straight to where we sat on the wooden porch swing outside the cottage doors. We noticed Don building a fire in the pit situated out past the house on the lawn near the beach entrance. Don sat down for a few minutes and I leaned over to James and encouraged him to go talk to Don. There was immediate and intense fear in my husband's eyes, something I was getting used to seeing in these tumultuous days. "I'm not sure he wants to talk to me," he said. So I proceeded to give him "the eye," which translated into me saying I wanted him to go whether he felt like it or not. I wasn't aware until later in our recovery process how consuming the shame factor is for people in James' situation. It is one of the aspects that makes moving forward so difficult. At that moment in time, however, it was just strange that I was urging my once confident and fearless husband to do something that always seemed so natural for him. Our normal dance consisted of him coaxing me out of the shadows. He reluctantly agreed and slowly walked across the grass toward Don.

I sat on the swing for a while watching James and Don talk. I could see James hang his head down, shaking it back and forth. After thirty minutes, I went inside with the girls. More time passed, and I got up and stood by the window that offered a view to the yard and beach. They were still huddled around that fire pit talking. I vividly recall thinking how beautiful that looked, just those two men out there talking. I couldn't remember the last time I saw my husband do such a thing. We were always running, ministering, teaching, driving, driving, driving. Sure, we met with people one on one, but it was always mingled with ministry. As you will read in future chapters, our deep hurts and wounds from the past created walls of protection, not allowing anyone into our lives beyond a certain point. Our walls were now obliterated, giving way to a painful, but authentic opportunity to know and be known.

It was when I was standing there looking out the window that the Lord blew the lid off my perception of ministry. I came to a new understanding of the true depth of relationship and how intensely important it is to transformation, health, and true discipleship. Don, his dog, and the generosity of his heart to open his doors, give of his time and attention, and listen and extend the love of Jesus to a broken family was profound. It was the palpable definition of the power of one. I could see with new eyes how being vulnerable in relationship from one to another can unleash exponential potential. I perceived that God was up to more than meets the eye with our little trip to the North Shore.

3:00 a.m. flashed on the clock by the bed in the room I was in by myself. It had become a normal thing for me to either be up until this hour or to have fallen asleep and wake up in the early morning and just lay there. I glanced around the room at the beautiful decor and wished I could be enjoying it more than I was under these circumstances. I looked at the Bible that lay beside the bed and stared at it for a while. It had become almost a part of me in these days of grief. I heard the faint voice of the Holy Spirit urge me to read the account of Samuel and the Ebenezer stone. "Then Samuel took a stone and set it up between Mizpah and Shen. He named it Ebenezer, saying, 'Thus far the Lord has helped us'" (1 Samuel 7:12).

Ebenezer, which means "the stone of help," was set up as a memorial or monument by Samuel signifying that the Lord had been faithful and a reminder that He would continue to be faithful in future need as the children of Israel walked in obedience to Him. This brought great comfort to my weary heart that early morning when my future seemed so daunting before me. I was reminded that God had truly been faithful to us as a family, as displayed in the simple fact that we were intact at that moment and in this beautiful place. I was given another infusion of hope that God would walk with us as we journeyed this unknown and battle–ridden road stretched out ahead of us. Just as Samuel was demonstrating for all to see, when he placed that stone of help in plain sight as a reminder that they served a steadfast God, it was also a call to expect the miracles he was confident the Lord would accomplish on their behalf in the days and years to come. I heard the Lord impress on my heart, "Take a stone from this place as a reminder and a future monument for your family."

I slept that night with my Bible firmly under my arm, like a child's blanket giving needed comfort. When I woke up, I stretched and felt that yucky tired you feel when you don't get enough sleep. As I sat up, I remembered the words the Lord imparted to my heart just a few hours prior. It gave me a boost of energy, and I opened the door of the room to see James and the girls preparing breakfast. Looking back, I can now verbalize the difficulty I was feeling, seeing my life the same, yet now so different. The people in my life were all there, yet it felt as if we were all damaged now, and I was unable in my power to repair it. I had begun the grieving process for the parts of my life that were just plain never going to be the same, while at the same time, hanging onto the hope that what the Lord would create would be somehow sweeter.

These are the moments when I am truly thankful for the loving words of encouragement from my Heavenly Father, because without them, I feel as if I might have imploded.

After a quiet family meal, I set out to find the perfect "stone of help," as recommended by the Lord. I walked around the large yard settling on a bed of black rocks near the steps of the cottage. There were stones of many sizes, some tiny and some bigger than my hand. I knew it needed to fit in my luggage for our final flight home to California in a month, so I focused my attention on the palm–sized stones near the flowerbed. I tossed a few around, then settled on a small stone that seemed the perfect size. I picked it up in my hand and rotated my palm up to see this monument and reminder the Lord had urged me to find. I uncurled my fingers and gasped. "No way," are the exact words that came out of my mouth as I caught a glimpse of the smooth, heart–shaped stone. Honestly, it might not have meant much to anyone else on the face of the earth, but for me, it was a perfect symbol of what was at stake and the kind of love being offered by our Savior as sustenance for our journey. Just to make sure I wasn't making a big deal out of nothing, I examined the rocks one more time to see if there were more that just happened to be perfectly shaped like a heart. Not one! I had the one that was meant for us.

When I told James of the Lord's prompting regarding the Ebenezer stone and showed him the one I grabbed, he began to cry. At that point, we couldn't even say a word between us because we were both sobbing. That little, black, heart-shaped stone has been with us every step of this pilgrimage. It currently sits beside our bed in plain sight for our family to remember whom we owe our hearts and lives to daily. It's been worn even smoother by our hands as we've held it frequently when the days and nights got really hard. When we've had to step out in faith—yet again—and risk the unknown, that little monument has been a comfort. It reminds us that Jesus is our Savior, our sufficiency, and the very hope for our future. It helps us remember that God gave us a do-over, a beautiful new beginning; and it started, for the most part, on that weekend at the North Shore.

I cried when it was time to leave that little cottage. I didn't want to go; the world seemed too big and scary in stark contrast to that lovely shelter in paradise. But we had to go, and I leaned once again on the shoulders of my Father, holding our Ebenezer stone in my hand. *God's got this*, I whispered to myself, and we drove home.

I am so thankful for that weekend, as the experience simply changed us and broke down walls that would have held back the transformative process that was about to take place through relationship and the healing touch of Jesus in the days, weeks, and months to come. God intervened and showed us love and hope again through His Word and through the kindness of another believer. If we ever make it back to that special place, you can be assured that we will be holding that Ebenezer stone, our stone of help. With hands held tightly together, we will declare the powerful and hard fought truth that, "Thus far the Lord has helped us!"

THE BEAUTY OF OHANA

James and I have always enjoyed long walks together. We've been taking evening walks ever since we were married at twenty years of age and finishing college together. We'd walk for miles, talking and dreaming about what life would be like when…and we'd fill in the blank. Our walks had become more sporadic in recent years, as life became busy and all consuming. We would be lucky if we got one or two good walks in a month. That may not seem like a huge issue, except it was our primary time to communicate. Then our world came crashing down, and all we had was time to communicate.

There we'd sit after dropping the kids off at school, just the two of us, staring at one another across the table in our townhome. It's a funny thing when you've lost everything. You start to look back at your life and remember what worked, because it's apparent in that moment what didn't. We realized that our walks were a very important part of our story. A good deal of our dreaming, praying, and conflict resolution occurred when we put on our running shoes and talked without interruption.

The island of Oahu is not short on beautiful places to walk, but we found our favorite spot to start this important tradition once again, along the beach in Waimanalo. The backdrop was gorgeous beyond description with crystal clear blue water rolling onto the warm and almost untouched sand. There were days I couldn't utter anything beyond a few words and other days when we'd cry together, and even laugh on occasion. Truth be told, there were many times I would just scream and flail my arms around for all to see. On one particular morning walk, we passed two men fishing along the shore. As we navigated around their fishing lines, I noticed the two peacefully enjoying each other's company. When we got back home, I entered these thoughts in my journal.

JOURNAL ENTRY MAY 10, 2013

It's a bright May morning. The world is teeming with life and beauty all around me, but my sadness runs so deeply I can hardly see it. My heart has been ripped out, our dreams have washed away, and I am left with the decision to take God at His word, walking forward in the hope He has extended, one excruciatingly difficult step at a time.

I am thinking a lot these days of the word and concept of "Ohana." In Hawaiian it means "family." I always smile when I remember my girls reciting the extended definition to me in their cute toddler voices after watching Disney's "Lilo and Stitch" some years ago. "Ohana means family, family means no one gets left behind or forgotten."

Once again this morning I was thinking of "Ohana" as we passed a man and what looked like his elderly father fishing along the beach in Waimanalo. They weren't saying much, and it didn't look like they had any fancy fishing equipment, but there was a richness and a contentment that was striking to me, a togetherness that was moving.

Oh, how I desire for the Lord to make evident to us in our hour of need this touch of "Ohana" that I've seen displayed over and over in the Hawaiian people. May it renew my hope that though I feel very alone and our family has suffered many losses, we are not left behind or forgotten.

The way we saw *Ohana* lived out among the Hawaiian people during our brief time living on Oahu was foundational to our healing journey. It was a tangible and substantive display of God's grace that softened our hearts and turned our tiny world upside down. In a broadened interpretation, Wikipedia says that *Ohana* includes the concepts of not only blood–related family members, but also adoptive and intentional members as well. In essence, it means that once we consider you family, you are family. Come rain or shine, we are here for you. Why does this make any difference in our daily lives? The truth is, it makes all the difference.

We will forever journey in a new way, thanks to our transformative experience with those who taught us firsthand what *Ohana* means. It makes us look differently at each other as a family unit. The mantra that says, "no one gets left behind or forgotten" can go a long way when we hike the lengthy and dusty trails of life together with all its ups and downs, twists and turns. But it also transformed the way we view those who journey in this world around us, those in close proximity to us, and even those who might be an ocean away. When we expand the concept of *Ohana* to encompass the family of God, then it's safe to say the same heart and grace applies.

If Paul takes the time to give praise in Ephesians 1:6 (NKJV) that God has "made us accepted in the Beloved," then we, too, are at peace knowing that we are part of God's *Ohana* when we ask Jesus into our hearts. The word "accepted" literally means "graced with grace" (Spirit Filled Life Bible). Life is no longer about just trying to make a living or simply evangelizing the world. It is about extending the hand of grace to others, knowing that we are all in the same boat. Without the redemptive blood of Jesus and His adoptive gift of grace, we would be nowhere.

It takes great love, time, effort, and long-suffering to live *Ohana*, which is why so many of us who have lived life at breakneck speeds have missed its essence altogether. It is intentional and empathetic. It goes beyond the superficial and stays the long haul. It looks at others' shortcomings through the eyes of Jesus and trusts, that though we all have difficult seasons, it's our Heavenly Father who ultimately brings healing in His timing. *Ohana* cares about your tomorrows enough to help carry you when you are broken and prays with real tears in the dark, scary nights. It gives when it hurts and is around long enough to rejoice when morning comes. It even opens its North Shore home and stays a while to "talk story."

Ohana means no one is left behind or forgotten. You, my friend who has decided to read this fragile story of our lives, may feel as if you are stranded on a distant shore completely overwhelmed by pain, fear, sin, tragedy, or doubt, and that you are the forgotten one. Please know that you are never out of the Lord's reach. You are never too far away to be graced with grace. I know. I understand. When it finally got deep down enough for me to comprehend with my whole heart that I am part of God's *Ohana* and nothing can change that, then I was free. I was free not only to be at peace in my own life and in all circumstances, but also to live out that peace and love in the world around me. What would the world look like if we all deeply understood and lived out this concept of *Ohana*? It's definitely something to think about.

Chapter 3

LET THE HEALING BEGIN

I was being drawn back to my first love, but this time it was in pure vulnerability and transparency of my truest self in Him…

I've always been curious about the heart of a first responder. What makes someone brave and courageous enough to step out when the risk is highest, the situation is most graphic and raw, and there is potential for personal loss? What kind of person willingly opens Pandora's Box and is strong and hopeful enough to assist in clearing away the chaos and debris?

The fearless first responders in our case came in the form of Dr. Ted and Diane Roberts of Pure Desire Ministries International. I remember the day Diane called me, kindly introduced herself, and asked how I was doing. Since I have lived so much of my life acting like everything is okay even when it's not, I started speaking to her with all the strong form and fashion a good woman in ministry can muster at any given moment. Diane saw right through it. She was kind and loving, but firm at the same time in regard to my health, honesty, and safety. (Newsflash: This is how I've always operated, and more often than not, I put my needs last on the to–do list.)

Personally, this day marked the beginning of a new journey for me that included getting real with how I was feeling. My hurt, pain, and anger was substantive and it had been there for a good portion of my life. I would no more, "grin and bear it," or give the good answer everyone wants to hear. My motivation had paramount significance, but lacked the ability to fix the heck out of everything around me.

James had a conversation with Dr. Ted Roberts, a pastor and leader of Pure Desire Ministries, that he had known for years. Dr. Ted laid the foundation of our strategy, meeting on a regular basis for a year of recovery and therapy in their program. We were required to take extensive, written clinical tests. The analysis of which would give them a better picture of what they were working with when they met with us for the first time.

It was both shocking and fascinating when we convened with them via video conference in mid May. I recall the two of us sitting together at the end of our bed upstairs in our townhome where the Internet connection was the strongest. It was strange and familiar to have been so close to my husband at that moment… surreal. It was like we were on the same team, wanting the same outcome, but not yet on the same page. What unfolded next was the most honest and striking look into the bowels of our lives that anyone, especially us, had ever dared go.

Dr. Ted and Diane started with James' analysis first. It showed him to be a very strong, motivated, and competent individual. "You are a man of high character," I heard Dr. Ted say directly to James. He quickly rejected Dr. Ted's statement, and said sharply, "I am not a man of character." I love the way God works, because it's just like our Father to put a strong man with another strong man and watch the sparks fly. Dr. Ted shot back in a firm, no–nonsense voice, "Stop speaking lies about yourself! You are a man of character; neither I, nor these tests, lie." Silence. I looked at James, then back at Dr. Ted on the computer screen, waiting to see what was going to happen next. I wasn't quite sure how my husband was going to respond to this interchange. To my surprise, he started to cry. It was a guttural cry from down deep inside where it had been covered up for years with the wreckage of a broken and wounded heart. Sadness filled me as I watched.

As the tears subsided, we moved on. They showed us the rest of the results. What was so incredibly striking was the fact that James' analysis showed very high levels of childhood trauma—trauma that had sat and seethed for decades. In other words, what was driving his behavior had been there since before he was ten years old. At this moment, something broke. It's hard to describe, but I believe the easiest way to look at it would be to picture Jesus extending his nail–scarred hand toward James and lovingly touching the scars that were inaccessible for so long. Those wretched scars and lies were being exposed as the underbelly of the pain that drove him to do things that were so far from the Lord's original plan for him and for our lives. It was like Jesus was saying, "Enough! Today you need to start to understand who you are in Me."

For all the anger I had toward my husband, I could recognize the Holy Spirit working carefully, like a skilled physician in open–heart surgery. The display was tender and poignant.

It doesn't matter what condition you are in when you see the Lord ministering to a damaged soul. If you allow your heart to be open even a fraction of a centimeter, you are changed by the encounter. There were, of course, no excuses made for the sinful behavior and hurt James had caused to others from his choices. But, for the first time in my husband's life, it was truth speaking to the source of his pain, not shame and worthlessness. As difficult and uncomfortable as it was to start the healing process when the devastation was so deep, it was like a breath of fresh air when we were given a valid plan to unhinge the enemy's longstanding stronghold.

My life was on display next. There were legitimate spikes in my analysis as well, but different kinds. My trauma came from a few childhood incidences and was then layered with many repetitive issues over time, thus creating a crater of hurt and pain that greatly affected my sense of worth. The analysis helped bring clarification that because I felt so bad about myself, I often overlooked things (pains, offenses, etc.) in my husband and others. A person who was less wounded would have confronted these years before. I remember Diane saying, "You did not cause this, Teri," filling my bruised and confused soul with relief and freedom. They took time to minister the love of Jesus to my broken and betrayed heart, and explained how refreshing it was to work with a wife who was so open to the process. "It can take many months to get a wife where you are today," Dr. Ted said kindly. I began to see in myself a strength I never knew existed.

Dr. Ted and Diane explained that trauma can come into our lives in either a *whack* or *lack* and that each is destructive in its own right. The *whack* occurs when severe circumstances or abuses are acutely thrust on us, and the *lack* occurs over time when we are traumatized by the absence of certain, fundamental emotional or physical needs. Either or both can cause severe wounds in a person's soul, and that person can be affected to varying degrees based on their individual response and tolerance. In other words, there is no way to estimate the impact of one situation or experience in comparison to the impact of another's life experience. Our response to any degree of trauma in our personal lives is as unique as our fingerprints.[2]

Up until this point in my life, I had no idea that I carried so much pain and anger around, like a backpack loaded with bricks. No wonder I always felt so drained and exhausted emotionally. I also had no idea that the woundedness of one person could cause so much damage in someone else's life. We were getting a glimpse of the battle plan we were accepting when we chose to get healing for our individual lives and for our marriage and family. It wasn't looking easy, and it was apparent that we were facing bondage that had been in place for generations. "Your pain level is going to increase," Dr. Ted explained to us, "You need to be ready for it."

Now that we were starting to identify the roots, it was going to take intense spiritual warfare, hard–core accountability, and a relentless commitment to follow the program if we wanted to see health, especially for James. There was no "fast food" option here. It was an "all in" kind of endeavor. I felt as if the fog was lifting just a bit, so we could at least see what direction our ship needed to set its course. Yet, the stormy seas ahead looked intimidating. Though clinical analysis had pinpointed the source, we were now charged with setting our hearts on the Lord to uproot and minister His healing touch to the specific wounds that drove our individual behaviors. This process would put us on a path to wholeness. Charles Stanley says it well, "Renewing the mind is a little like refinishing furniture. It is a two–stage process. It involves taking off the old and replacing it with the new. The old is the lies you have learned to tell or were taught by those around you; it is the attitudes and ideas that have become

---

2   Rebecca Bradley & Diane Roberts, *Behind the Mask: Authentic Living for Young Women* (Gresham, OR: Pure Desire Ministries International, 2012) 76–77.

a part of your thinking but do not reflect reality. The new is the truth. To renew your mind is to involve yourself in the process of allowing God to bring to the surface the lies you have mistakenly accepted and replace them with truth."[3]

We discovered that for each trauma or loss we had suffered in life, we had taken up a lie or made a vow in order to survive. For James, that occurred very early in the foundation of his person, making it almost fused to him; though it was never who he was in Christ, he couldn't tell the difference. So for the entirety of his life journey, he felt shame and worthlessness and believed that to be foundational truth. When a lie is that deep in a person's brain, it is impossible to eradicate without the power of the Holy Spirit. For a person to experience any lasting freedom, the lie must be identified and replaced with God's powerful truth.

Likewise, I had suffered a long list of circumstances that conditioned me to seek safety before any other need. Unknowingly being taken through the addictive cycle of my husband, which included bouts of anxiety, anger, and isolation, increased my fear. This cycle, which repeated itself every few months, or more frequently when stress was high, brought great confusion and hurt, making my need for safety even more intense. Our situation did not include any physical abuse or severe emotional abuse, but more a confusion on my part about my husband seeming so burdened at times, but unable to talk about it. He was never able to connect the dots regarding his inner pain and early childhood experiences.

These silent, subterranean conflicts going on inside both of us caused arguments and angry outbursts, driving our pain deeper and separating us from each other one inch at a time, until we had walked miles apart in certain areas of our relationship. I

---

3   Charles F. Stanley, *A Touch of His Freedom: Meditations on Freedom in Christ* (Grand Rapids, MI: Zondervan, 1991) 27–28.

mistakenly believed that at the end of the day, I was the only one who could be depended on to keep things going. Because I had such a low sense of worth, it created a roller coaster of control and disappointment that infected my soul and diminished my voice. We were the perfect storm, if you will, for the enemy's lifelong plan to take two gifted and anointed individuals and lead them to utter destruction.

I think we slept for two days after our first session in May. We were emotionally and physically exhausted. We were given daily homework and were asked to join an accountability group. For James, this was a Pure Desire group for men, and for me, it was a Betrayal & Beyond group for women. Quite a few people have asked me how I made it through those first difficult and isolated weeks after finding out about my husband's behavior and choices. When I think back to the early stages of recovery and read through my journals, it is clear that my dependence on the Lord was at an all–time high. It's the undeniable truth that, "The Lord is close to the brokenhearted and saves those who are crushed in spirit" (Psalm 34:18). Only someone who has walked through the valley can say "amen" to that one, and mean it with every fiber of their being. In a very real sense, Jesus became my husband. I had to let go of any and all control regarding how James would ultimately respond to the therapy, take ownership of my part, and let the Lord do the rest.

Above all else, I began to hear my Heavenly Father's voice in my head. He was replacing the voices from the past, one whisper at a time, until our closeness was so crazy amazing that it was my top priority. Everything else just flowed from it. My Daddy God was delivering me from a lifetime of lies and fears, and imparting His truth, thereby making me into a new person. I was being reconciled back to Him from the unhealthy path I had journeyed on for years. I was being drawn back to my first love, but this time it was in pure vulnerability and transparency of my truest self in Him.

The words of 2 Corinthians 5:17 rang true to the deepest part of my soul, "Therefore, if anyone is in Christ, the new creation has come: The old has gone, the new is here!" This time of recovery and place of dependence will always be special to me, because, in spite of the chaos, I found a peace and presence that felt as close to heaven on earth as I have ever experienced. I laid my burdens down and found new life in the process. This new life was special and sacred; regardless of what the future held, I knew I would carry this with me for the rest of my life.

The other very important factor was our commitment to staying current with assignments given to us by Dr. Ted and Diane. The only way I can fully describe the program with Pure Desire Ministries is that it is comprehensive. It takes into consideration the struggling addict and the spouse, as well as the family. The curriculum is effective; though it is hardcore, it is worth every second. When we made a discovery or a breakthrough, it was Dr. Ted and Diane who rejoiced with us. If relapse occurred, (meaning James attempted to medicate the intense pain and shame he felt inside through finding some escape via the Internet) or when we had conflict, they intervened.

Diane helped me set proper boundaries for our family during recovery and prayerfully assisted me in making a safety plan during those first difficult months. This safety plan brought tough love to our fragile situation and gave real and tangible consequences for behavior, with which I was uncomfortable. For relapse, anger outbursts, lies, etc., there were agreed upon consequences that had to be followed in order to steer us into healthy living. In the next chapter, I will go into greater detail about the destruction a process addiction can create. At this point, let me interject that it takes an average of ninety days to see those destructive patterns brought under control. Someone who has lived with an addiction knows that lies and isolation can seem natural.

This understanding took some time for me to grasp. I was too shocked at first to even consider that my husband of twenty years was capable of lying; the truth was, he didn't lie about any other aspect of his life. He had learned from the time he was a young child to compartmentalize his world into neat little boxes. The compartment that contained this shameful part of his life (his coping behavior) was off limits, and he protected it with deception—a behavior he used to survive his formative years. To walk in health, there must be truth and accountability. When that is compromised, the pain on the outside must exceed the pain on the inside in order for the person to get to their breaking point or "rock bottom," which ultimately helps them snap out of the pattern. This is where consequences come into play.

For our situation, James was very receptive and put every ounce of his effort into the process. This made implementing a safety plan easier. If he relapsed, he would incur a two week consequence of sleeping on the floor. If he lied regarding relapse or told me after twenty–four hours, then the consequence was greater. The safety plan included a list of situations and range of consequences, all the way up to his being asked to leave our home. This may sound severe, but it was necessary for the first crucial months to create an environment of safety for our family, as well as jump–start the recovery needed in his life. Believe me when I say it was one of the most difficult challenges of my life to learn all this information, put it into practice, stay strong, not cave in, and hang in there when things got messy. And honestly, things did get messy on numerous occasions.

If the foundation of addiction is how someone learned to medicate pain, then relearning takes some trial and error, but the family unit must be kept safe at all times. That is why it is crucial when going through this kind of recovery that you are knit closely into a program like Pure Desire. They became our lifeline. Thankfully, because of our intense dedication to this difficult path of recovery, we witnessed a miracle in James' life within that three–month period of breaking the bondage of pornography. For a man who spent most of his life in chains, freedom and liberty are now his life's rhythm.

Our girls were very aware of the process. There wasn't much we could have done otherwise. Their dad was a high–profile, influential pastor preaching to over 10,000 people one weekend, and was asked to step down from his position the next. There was no way around the truth and aftermath of the situation. From my perspective now, I realize that though it was extremely difficult, the absolute transparency of the circumstances helped our family realize the depth of consequences that can come from sinful choices. It also helped us all cling to God's grace for our survival, thus releasing the potential for a complete work of restoration for our family as a whole from the generational patterns that existed.

Watching our girls navigate this tragic situation was the most difficult thing we have ever experienced. I cannot describe the sadness they felt when many of their friends simply vanished, some of whom they have never seen again. Leaders who were in their lives when their daddy was being promoted to new levels of ministry just moved on. For our girls, it was like a wasteland of relationships that ended in confusion and disappointment. We began to understand that healing was needed as deeply in their little hearts as it was in ours, and once again we had to take one day at a time, love them unconditionally, and let God direct our path.

Our sole purpose as their parents became recovery and restoration through God's mighty hand and seeing the same for our girls. The Lord was making it glaringly apparent that if we are unhealthy, to any degree whether great or small, our legacy is at stake. And our most important legacy is our girls. Therefore, we decided that all our strength, time, and effort would be to that crucial end.

The verbiage and details regarding the situation were, and still are, age appropriate. We have been very careful to protect our girls from as much of the stress and unnecessary details that unfolded in each stage of the recovery and restoration as we possibly could. As a family, we have been vigilant to talk and pray constantly regarding what any of us are feeling, where God is in all of it, and what we are hoping and believing for in Christ for the future.

I remember calling Diane early in the recovery process and crying because we were dealing with an issue I felt we had already handled. I was originally trained as an elementary teacher, so my mind sees things very sequentially. When you finish one task, then you move on to the next. So, when we were back to what seemed like square one with an aspect of our relationship or old patterns of communication, I would flip out. She lovingly explained to me that this type of healing doesn't happen in clear levels like I was used to as a teacher, where you graduate from one grade level and never revisit it again, but rather in circles. On the next page is a diagram Diane gave me and her words of explanation.

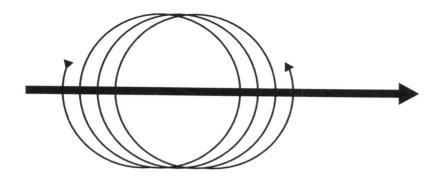

Because the healing process often occurs in layers or stages, a majority of the healing experience will not be a straight–line improvement upward and onward. Rather, most people cycle several times through the stages of the healing process, as shown in the diagram. At times it may feel like you are regressing, but often God uses the recycling process to reveal the hidden source and patterns which ultimately give you a deeper understanding of the issue with which you have been struggling.[4]

4   Diane Roberts (Gresham, OR: Pure Desire Ministries International, 2014).

Sometimes we don't allow healing to take place in a particular area and so we find ourselves in the same place once again. But overall, it's just a matter of God's patience with us, which He has in abundance. He knows we have deep wounds that harbor great pain and so, He may take us into the place of our wound only so deep the first time through. The next time He takes us a little deeper, and even deeper the next time, and so on. Healing is a process, and our Father is a patient healer.

"Yippee," I said, sarcastically, as I thought about the repetitious nature of the process, "we get to do it again!" What I came to understand as we journeyed further into healing is that as we began to get real with our issues; health and truth were replacing pain and lies, giving us more strength to go back and deal with the really deep baggage we left behind or simply didn't want to pick up. But it was a process, and still is.

This concept of healing circles has helped us immensely in our recovery and will be of great benefit for years to come. When we find ourselves hitting a wall repeatedly regarding a particular issue, we now stop, talk about it as a couple or a family, and realize God is allowing us to go back and circle until we can get free in Him. It's not scary; it doesn't derail us or zap our hope like it did in the beginning. Rather, it tells us to push in, pray earnestly, seek our Father, and get honest about what is driving our behavior.

We know that we will have to circle with our girls for the rest of our lives in one way or another as we experience new circumstances along the way. It is our privilege and honor to guide them in such endeavors. When they come to difficult seasons, we will be honest about what they went through in their childhood. When it is time for them to get married, have children of their own, or any situation that may require a circle or two, you can count on the fact that we will lovingly be there to guide them through it.

Wholeness is not attained at a one–stop–shop. We traverse this life with healing opportunities all around us, and though we have seasons where it is the main focus—like our recent past— we must come to terms with the fact that in order to go from "glory to glory" (2 Corinthians 3:18 NKJV) we must be open to continual healing from the Lord. If not, our most important legacy is at stake. The beautiful reality is that this perspective and understanding also gives us a more gracious view of others as they circle in the process of wholeness as well, knowing that God is ultimately in control.

I'll wrap up this chapter with the words of Isaiah 61, which became a light to our path in our darkest hour. I remember hearing the Lord direct me to read it out loud over our marriage and our family in those difficult, early days of our recovery; when the future was as uncertain and foreboding, as the rocky shores of home hidden by dense fog in the still of the night. Isaiah 61 became a lighthouse that beckoned us onward and highlighted the illuminating possibilities found in Jesus. Wherever you are in your healing journey, I pray it will be a light to you as well.

ISAIAH 61

¹ *The Spirit of the Sovereign Lord is on me,*
because the Lord has anointed me
to proclaim good news to the poor.
He has sent me to bind up the brokenhearted,
to proclaim freedom for the captives
and release from darkness for the prisoners,

² *to proclaim the year of the Lord's favor*
and the day of vengeance of our God,
to comfort all who mourn,

³ *and provide for those who grieve in Zion—*
to bestow on them a crown of beauty
instead of ashes,
the oil of joy
instead of mourning,
and a garment of praise
instead of a spirit of despair.
They will be called oaks of righteousness,
a planting of the Lord
for the display of his splendor.

⁴ *They will rebuild the ancient ruins*
and restore the places long devastated;
they will renew the ruined cities
that have been devastated for generations.
⁵ *Strangers will shepherd your flocks;*
foreigners will work your fields and vineyards.
⁶ *And you will be called priests of the Lord,*
you will be named ministers of our God.
You will feed on the wealth of nations,

and in their riches you will boast.
⁷ Instead of your shame
you will receive a double portion,
and instead of disgrace
you will rejoice in your inheritance.
And so you will inherit a double portion in your land,
and everlasting joy will be yours.

⁸ "For I, the Lord, love justice;
I hate robbery and wrongdoing.
In my faithfulness I will reward my people
and make an everlasting covenant with them.

⁹ Their descendants will be known among the nations
and their offspring among the peoples.
All who see them will acknowledge
that they are a people the Lord has blessed."

¹⁰ I delight greatly in the Lord;
my soul rejoices in my God.
For he has clothed me with garments of salvation
and arrayed me in a robe of his righteousness,
as a bridegroom adorns his head like a priest,
and as a bride adorns herself with her jewels.

¹¹ For as the soil makes the sprout come up
and a garden causes seeds to grow,
so the Sovereign Lord will make righteousness
and praise spring up before all nations.

Chapter 4

MY BELOVED

As humans we are wounded in community,
and we are also healed in community.

When Dr. Ted told us that the pain level was going to increase, he wasn't kidding. This was especially true for James as he fought to take back control of his mind. I exaggerate not when I say that if one chooses to take on this battle, it cannot be done with half a heart. It will rock you and your spouse to the core.

On one particular day near the end of May, as I sat surrounded by mountains of brown, moving boxes and the clutter of packing material strewn around our townhome, I felt a little like one of our dishes all wrapped up tightly in the dark, stuffy box, marked "fragile." The voyage ahead was not an easy one, and the unknown was, frankly, unnerving to me. Our life began to display the faint echoes of a love story mingled with the hard edges of a Greek tragedy. "What is to become of our family and all this stuff, Lord? All these possessions don't mean as much as they used to in relation to the disaster we have thus far survived. Though I'm starting to understand some of the 'why' behind what happened, I'm burdened under the weight of feeling both compassion and anger toward my husband." My words to the Lord spilled out amid the boxes. "I know, the path that leads to a life free of bitterness is found in You. I need to see my husband through Your eyes, Jesus. You are the only way we can make it through this."

I leaned my head against the box next to me, as I sat crisscross on the floor and waited for a while. "My beloved has lost his way and I want you to walk with him," the Lord whispered to me in my desperation. I lifted my eyes up beyond the disarray of boxes and out toward our lanai where I heard the cooing of our two regular visitors, the pair of doves our girls had named Romeo and Juliet. These two birds sat there every single day, rain or shine, huddled together on the railing that overlooked our dock. There they were again, against all odds, braving the elements, stuck together like glue. I stared at them for a while and sighed, then my mind drifted back to the words the Lord had just spoken to my heart.

"That's how you see James, as Your beloved?" I questioned back. Honestly, in all the crazy chaos and pain, I forgot that the pure love of Christ toward James was unhindered by our present circumstances. Jesus was helping me see this man, not only in terms of my fractured relationship with him, but in the heavenly light of eternity and his connection with the King of Kings. I felt as if my Daddy God was reassuring me that James was ultimately His and my part was complementary to His great love. From that day until the present, when the Lord refers to James in my heart, it is always as "beloved." I can't explain why that is the case, but I know for a fact that it has brought great peace to me when I wanted to pick up an offense or forget the importance of our true identity to our Heavenly Father.

It's easy to view people solely in terms of what they have done in the past instead of who they are to the Father and where they ultimately belong—worshiping God in Heaven, our real home. When we start seeing things in an eternal light, the really hard stuff here on earth loses some of its sting, releasing Jesus to touch our wounds and wash away the dirty residue that holds us back from clearly steering toward the real goal. I wasn't excusing behavior or turning a blind eye, but rather looking at my husband through Jesus. My limited and human perspective was being broadened to include the unseen heart and workings of a Holy God displayed to the object of His affection.

Simply put, there was something profound the Lord was doing in both our lives that would make a better "us" in the end, but it had to start with both of us coming to grips with who we belonged to individually. Knowing how the Lord viewed James, and me, for that matter, regardless of our temporal circumstances, brought a greater depth of understanding about the true nature of the God we serve. It freed me as I navigated the very hard days when it would have been easier to walk in the flesh and in the moments I was triggered by memories and anger. I'd like to say I never lashed out or flung a hurtful word or two in his direction (truthfully, I struggled deeply), but having this loving perspective helped me recognize when I moved outside of God's best for me and those around me.

I remember looking into James' eyes after we prayed and did our devotions in the morning together. I was moved by the shame and brokenness that poured out in dripping tears, like that of a lost little boy. I thought to myself, *How did he get so far from home?* It was apparent that though he lived for so long in this pain and sin, he didn't want to. He'd tell me in our newfound vulnerable moments how desperately he wanted freedom, but couldn't stop the madness. When the stresses of life and ministry began to substantially increase in the previous three years, he'd gotten to the point of trying to figure out a way to just end it all, somehow thinking that would be better for our family. I began to understand how that kind of desperation could leave a person open and susceptible to the unthinkable. At times, I wondered why he just couldn't come out with the truth, confess, and ask for help. That was when Dr. Ted and Diane began to open our eyes to what was happening inside James' brain neurologically, as well as spiritually.

At first glance, it may seem hard to believe that we could have ministered for so many years and not come to this place on our own. Some of it is still a mystery to me. However, the restoration process and the information we have received in the area of addiction and marriage recovery has brought new insight to us about the amazing intricacies of the brain and patterning that takes place, especially in our childhood from our family of origin, that can have lasting negative effects if not dealt with. But, it has also brought us to a new vulnerability and authenticity in our relationship with the Lord. We both sensed for years we needed help individually and as a couple, but felt trapped in the mindset that Christian leaders must be perfect. We were stuck in the perception that getting counseling is a sign of weakness. This might seem crazy, but when we started to talk to other Christian friends and leaders, the same thought process was present in them as well. Interesting…and something to think about in the context of the statistical evidence that over half of the pastors and leaders in America are in the very same situation we were, and not getting help for it.[5]

In the early weeks and months of our recovery, I often sat in bed and wondered why it all hadn't come apart earlier when

---

5   Jeremy & Tiana Wiles, Conquer Series: The Battle Plan for Purity, DVD 1 (West Palm Beach, FL: Kingdomworks Studios, 2013) conquerseries.com.

fewer lives were at stake, when the merry–go–round was moving slower and we could have just hopped off. I've come to realize that it's not that simple when the depth of pain and addictive patterning is so deep. Add to that the enemy's destructive plots and the depravity that sin produces, and it no longer becomes a merry–go–round you are trying to hop off of, but a fire–spitting meteor plummeting at 50,000 miles per hour. It's a lot harder to exit the latter.

Am I making justification for sin? Absolutely not! Sin is sin, and the Bible is very clear that the wages of sin is death (Romans 6:23)—death to the partaker and a ripple effect of death that goes outward to others as well. I can attest to that truth with blood, sweat, and tears. What I am bringing to the forefront, however, is the knowledge of what we have learned the hard way on this journey. Pain is real and when it's deep, the person in pain seeks to medicate that pain. It's the way our brains have been formed. The issue becomes what we are trained to seek as a means of medication. If we are taught to authentically and vulnerably seek God and are shown that in authenticity and vulnerability in healthy relationships we can find healing, then we have a fighting chance (Romans 12:2).

Contrary to this healthy way of dealing with pain and trauma is opting to "stay strong," which is what we typically do, where we forgo authenticity and vulnerability. Parents model that pattern to their children who, like my husband from a very young age, are then sucked into the vortex of societal, peer, and media–driven pressures as means of medicating the pain.

As you may remember from the last chapter, James suffered from childhood trauma. He was raised in a Christian home with parents who loved him, but had their own pain and generational issues they were trying to deal with the best they could. Little

James was being shown Christian values, but at the same time, he was witnessing his mom struggling with a pain medication addiction, his father dealing with inward anger, and a home that was a mix of love, shame, and volatility. All this was going on and no one talked to him about it. James was the youngest, so escaping and compartmentalizing was his way of coping when neglected or hurt. His mother started taking pain mediation after a back surgery when he was very young. James began to believe that he was the cause of his mom's pain and addictive behavior, as a result of misunderstood and overheard conversations.

In his little world of feeling shame and worthlessness, he thought that if he performed well, he would be okay and everyone would love and accept him—even God. This, in turn, began to shape the reward pathways in his brain to remember this kind of patterning and repeat when needed. All the while, the inner conflict and outward circumstances were producing greater and greater amounts of anger, driving him to make unhealthy vows to never let anyone beat him at anything again and under no circumstances, allow himself to cry ever again.

Please understand my heart when I say that we love his family dearly and realize that they would never intentionally cause pain and hurt. We have walked through a process of forgiveness and reconciliation with them, knowing they were just passing down the patterning and trauma–filled experiences that were a real part of their past as well. We learned that it's not about blaming, but identifying, renouncing, and walking through a process of healing and forgiveness, thereby releasing God's power on our family to break the generational issues that existed.

Enter the crazy world of preteen curiosity and peer pressure, and that moment when a friend introduced James to pornography. It may seem a simple act, but the more research that is done on brains exposed to pornographic images, the more people realize its devastating effects. Pornography lights up parts of the brain that frankly nothing else can, and releases chemicals in the brain similar to drugs. So, for all intents and purposes, young James' brain, which was already patterned toward compartmentalization and improper patterning for dealing with pain, got an imprint that it remembered as a valid means to numb and escape. As James' life progressed and stresses increased, the pain and shame deepened and intensified. Simultaneously, the enemy began to push in stronger, bringing more isolation. This is when his brain remembered the chemical imprint made on his reward pathway, and he was hooked.

The fact is, the neurochemistry of a person who has medicated their pain through a process addiction, like pornography has been changed from its original wiring. Viewing porn deceives a person's brain into responding similarly to a brain that has been exposed regularly to cocaine. So, the bottom line is that your brain can't tell the difference between porn and cocaine.[6] Therefore, over a period of time, the release of those pleasure chemicals actually alters the brain; in order for someone to even feel normal, they need to medicate more frequently and with greater intensity. Madness indeed![7]

I watched and prayed as my husband took his life back one tiny step at a time with the help of the Lord. I had no doubt in my mind that the Lord was working a miracle of great proportion in James. Like many people who decide to find freedom from this issue, James had to relearn a pattern of healthy living, as well as undergo spiritual transformation. It's a dual process. As a family,

---

6 fightthenewdrug.org

7 Ted & Diane Roberts, Pure Desire Ministries International, Gresham, OR. puredesire.org

we put proper safeguards on all our electronic devices that were connected to the internet. James and I were relentless with our communication regarding trigger points and weak moments. In the beginning months, I witnessed him weeping on his knees, asking God to help him take back control of his mind and walk in health for the sake of his wife and his girls.

At times, I wasn't sure he was ever going to recover. It was like living with someone who was coming off drugs, but with bags of the stuff sitting around everywhere. You don't have to look far in any given website, phone app, TV program, billboard advertisement, or magazine at the grocery store to see something that can take a fragile brain down a destructive path.

I am sure you, like me, have accidentally clicked on a website that brought up images you were not expecting. I'd been so naive in the past, not taking a more offensive stance on the deluge of toxic messages and images pervading our society. There are children, teens, and young adults walking daily in our midst who are trapped and addicted to pornography. These priceless boys and girls are holding their deceiver and the weapon being used to destroy their lives in their back pocket, and it's as if no one is paying attention. I know I wasn't, for the most part. I believed that it was only a moral issue. I thought just saying "don't," "it's bad," and "it's evil," would deter any "good" person from such behavior, and turning my nose up to anything or anyone associated with it was natural. In my perfectly imperfect world I'd hurl off comments like, "Who could ever do such a thing?" or "What's wrong with a person who looks at that stuff?" Then I sat perplexed, contemplating why a person of any age wouldn't feel free or comfortable coming out and asking for help from a legitimate issue that not only suffocates them spiritually, but also has changed their neurochemistry in the process.

I am not in any way saying, however, that media, electronics, or smartphones are bad or inherently evil. I have the latest electronic devices at my fingertips, and I use them on a daily basis. It's how these devices are used that changes everything. It's how we protect ourselves against the onslaught meant to derail us that matters. If, statistically, well over half of the men in our society, with women following close behind, anonymously admit to struggling with this issue to the point of addiction, yet no one admits to anything publicly, we must allow the Holy Spirit room to work in our hearts as to why. The sobering truth is that those of us who've gone before are patterning the next generation. Are we modeling vulnerability and authenticity to them, laying the groundwork for freedom in their lives? Their world is media–driven; it's their first language. While many of us have grown into it, electronic media has been an integral part of their lives; for that very reason, it is much more difficult for them to get free of its misuse than those of us who have lived part of life without it. We must ask ourselves, if we really care at all, are we providing safe environments for precious people to step out of the shadows and get free? Are we aware of the real dangers that exist, and are we brave enough to start a loving discussion?

Jesus is very clear that He came for the lost, the broken, the bruised, and the blind. He had great compassion for the sinner, the wounded, the deceived, the diseased, and the orphaned. His response to all of them was "come." Once I began to see with new eyes the wasteland produced because of this issue, I wanted people to understand. Unfortunately, the response I most commonly got from others when I brought up anything to do with pornography or sexual addiction was much like that of my former self, judgmental and shame–based. Heartbreaking…

There was, however, a man in all his brokenness, choosing every day to push back the enemy's onslaught; despite the hurling insults and shameful rhetoric, he pressed on. James would wake up early, do his devotions, then his Pure Desire homework. We'd walk and talk, we'd cry, and talk some more. James had to come to terms with the deep wounds that drove his behavior and begin to live his life free of compartments and secrecy. Dr. Ted told us something that made sense as we journeyed this excruciatingly difficult path: as humans we are wounded in community, and we are also healed in community. Granted, our community at this point in time was very small, but it was enough for the Lord to do His finest work in our lives. When an issue of pain or hurt arose, I observed a wounded man choose the hard thing, which was to deal with it through vulnerability and transparency. He called or texted his accountability group, Dr. Ted, or our pastor with things that may seem small to most people, but to him, could trigger hurt and shame to the point of relapse.

I remember watching him rediscover who he was in Christ, like a person who comes to the Lord for the first time—wide-eyed and awed by the wonder and possibility of a frail and fractured human heart in the hand of Jehovah Rapha, the Lord who heals. In a very real sense, I was watching an illustrated sermon of 2 Corinthians 10:3–5. The Message version says it beautifully:

The world is unprincipled. It's dog-eat-dog out there! The world doesn't fight fair. But we don't live or fight our battles that way—never have and never will. The tools of our trade aren't for marketing or manipulation, but they are for demolishing that entire massively corrupt culture. We use our powerful God-tools for smashing warped philosophies, tearing down barriers erected against the truth of God, fitting every loose thought and emotion and impulse into the structure of life shaped by Christ. Our tools are ready at hand for clearing the ground of every obstruction and building lives of obedience into maturity.

I don't know your name, where you live, your background, or your socio–economic status. I'm not privy to the details of your daily routine or the hurts and wounds that may exist in your life. I do, however, know that there is a God who calls you His beloved. Beloved. Just pause for a moment and let that sink in. The creator of the universe is head–over–heels in love with you...and regardless of your baggage, your history, or your present predicaments, He calls you His own. I've come to a new understanding of that love as witnessed in my husband's life. It is a rare and precious love that takes the time to pick up the shattered and pulverized pieces of a life, a life many would and did write off, and painstakingly put them back together to create a masterpiece. That love is calling out to you, His beloved son or daughter. You may have read this testimony and come to the realization that you need help. Please know that there is hope, and as I found out that day in April, it can compel you to take one step at a time toward a life of freedom. Don't give up hope.

I also realize that there are those reading this who may be provoked to anger, sadness, or even great compassion. The issue of pornography is a real and present danger to the beautiful people all around you. It's a vacuum that sucks the life out of those caught in its deadly web—the consumer, those involved in its production, and many innocent bystanders. I know it's hard to hear and a little hard to write, but the judgment and shame surrounding these issues in the church are very high.

My husband is living proof of the conflict many feel and the devastation lurking in the shadows. If we do not combat this issue, what is to become of the next generation? We cannot be naive in thinking this issue is going to just go away when the use of technology is increasing exponentially.

As the body of Christ, we have an important opportunity to live out the kind of love and relationship for which Jesus died. Can we be honest with ourselves and step out to provide a safe place for people in their struggles and then walk with them into freedom? The harsh reality is that the secrecy surrounding pornography use and its ease of accessibility make the youth—especially the Christian youth—of our nation very susceptible to this type of coping behavior.

My friend, it's time to wake up before more lives are ruined.

So if the Son sets you free, you will be free indeed.
John 8:36

If you are interested in starting a discussion regarding the issues stated in this chapter, please join us at TheNovusProject.com.

Chapter 5

WHEN ALL OTHER
LIGHTS GO OUT

There was nothing left to grasp or hold onto,
but the light of God's Word and the bright echoes
of His love in the innermost part of my heart.

As a point of transparency, I am going to admit that I am a fan of the *Lord of the Rings* epic saga written by J.R.R. Tolkien. Ok, maybe "fan" is too light a term. I have been known to pull out the extended DVD version on more occasions than I can conceivably count. It is, of course, a literary masterpiece, but what has drawn me to revisit its storyline time and time again is the complex interaction of the characters and their journey amidst the evil trying to overtake the good for which they stand. I've always tried to identify myself with the beautiful heroine, Arwen; after all, she wears beautiful gowns and becomes queen in the end, right? However, I've come to embrace the fact that my life journey to date and hence forward more closely resembles that of Frodo and trustworthy Sam. This duo faces insurmountable odds and for a task not many would enlist. Their lives are woven together with loyalty, faith, and hope as their armor, as they take on the dark world thrust upon them.

I am drawn to the scene in which all the leaders of Middle Earth are arguing over who is going to take the "one ring" to its place of destruction. I relate whole-heartedly when Frodo speaks up and says, "I'll take it…though I do not know the way." How fresh in my mind comes the memory of the days during this process I felt the same. "Yes, Lord, this is not what I expected out of life. It's terribly scary and unknown, and where You are asking me to journey will likely have no royal procession to mark the path, but only the faint and solitary footsteps of a few who walk in faith, hoping that somehow there is something greater beyond the foreboding hills and valleys before us. But none the less, lead on."

I know my words are not lost on you, precious soul, who has felt the same way. You may have asked the same metaphorical question: "Wait a second, Lord, I auditioned for the role of the hero (or heroine). I think something got crossed in the casting department because You gave me the Hobbit costume with the torn up jacket and hairy feet; that's not what I auditioned for. I was waiting on my kingly sword (or the chiffon number that flows elegantly with each regal step). Maybe there's been some mistake?"

Dear friend, as I ponder the mysterious ways of the Lord, His sovereignty, and His unconditional love, all of which are beyond my human comprehension, I would be amiss if I didn't say I'm still a work in progress and I struggle at times trying to wrap my arms around it all. What I can say with a stout and earnest heart is this: for each and every place in my life since I've been walking with Jesus, I've found myself saying, "This isn't what I signed up for." I've tried to push in toward Him, and each time He answered with something words cannot describe. To be fair, there have been seasons it has taken me some measure of time to get to that place, but one way or another, get there I did. I guess that's why when the biggest challenge I have ever faced was laid at my feet, I could say, "I'll take it, Lord, but I don't know the way; you'll have to show me," and I meant it with all my heart, knowing He would be my faithful guide.

I'm not in any way implying that I am a super Christian or that I have not wrestled with deep conflict in many of my life's moments, but I guess at the end of the day there is something so foundational about that place, even if it's small and faint, that says, "Daddy, I'm here. Show me" (Proverbs 3:5–6), then waking up the next day and saying the same thing again, and so on and so on. For me, the great paradox came when I realized, that though I came as a child to Him when faced with difficult circumstances, I was still not completely free of the baggage and fears that wreaked havoc on my soul ever since I was a little girl.

When we are tasked with the process of uprooting the deep and dark wounds and patterns of the past, it is much like a journey through the treacherous lands of Middle Earth as depicted in Tolkien's *Lord of the Rings*; one minute you can feel like you're making headway along a breathtakingly beautiful path, and the next you're being ambushed by evil creatures trying to take your very life. It is a profound truth that we travel differently when we understand who we are in Christ. We walk confidently, not fearfully, in the gifts and strengths the Lord gave us. It is also true that it makes for a grueling journey when we travel burdened and confused. In this new process, I began to understand the very important point that God never changes His love or distance to us in our journey. He is still there, available, but how we travel through this life and through its trials is directly affected by our level of freedom in Him. That choice is ours.

How many believers meander in their lives like I did, limping along with the Lord, not fully grasping the true power and value of their individual existence and purpose in Him? Maybe you can relate to how I used to view life. I could easily encourage others to powerfully take on the demons that stood before them, but when it came to me, I just kind of shriveled up. It wasn't until I had someone to help me with the "why" questions, that I could see past the thick fog that shrouded my understanding, slowed me down, and skewed my view.

I wrote the following words in third person, as if I was looking at my life through a camera lens. It was one of the exercises I was asked to do in our journey of recovery. To be candid, at first I thought it was a silly task, but being the conscientious student that I am, I wasn't going to let an assignment get the best of me. I figured, *if I'm going to do this, I'm going all the way.* I prepared by taking a few days to pray and allow the Lord to soften my heart and unearth anything I was holding back or had walled up. Once I began writing, I couldn't stop. It was as if I'd been waiting a lifetime to get these words out of my soul and onto the page.

Once upon a time there was a little girl named Teri, who had a big heart and an even bigger imagination. The world around her was a place of amazing possibility and wonder, and much like Anne, in "Anne of Green Gables," which happened to be her favorite book, she was always asking questions, creating stories, and finding beauty in almost everything she saw. The world turned out to be a very different place than she had experienced early in her childhood. Fear came into her life, like a terrible storm, leaving her conflicted between her joy-filled, easy-going playtime and the foreboding dark clouds that lingered in the distance. She noticed that her family, though very loving to her, wasn't always as happy as she once perceived. Though they enjoyed many wonderful family memories, she would on occasion see her parents fight in the evenings, most commonly Wednesday nights when her daddy would go bowling. These nights became stressful to her because her mommy would leave late in the evening to pick him up after he'd been drinking. Teri began to fear that something terrible would happen to them both and she would be left all alone. Wednesday nights were full of dread.

Along came a friend who lived down the street. She would invite Teri, who was now ten years old, to her house to play. She seemed kind at first, but when the girls disagreed about what game to play or Teri wanted to leave early because she felt unsafe, the girl hit and scratched her, tore her clothes, and locked her in the closet for long periods of time. She threatened to hurt Teri if she ever told anyone what was happening. This went on for quite some time, with the physical and mental abuses against Teri escalating.

One day, Teri was riding her bike home. She turned to wave goodbye and slammed into the curb. She flipped over her bike, hitting her head on the street. When she got up, she saw she was bleeding badly and called to the other little girl for help, who responded by laughing, turning, and walking away, leaving Teri to crawl home. That was the last day Teri ever went to that little girl's house. She never told anyone what went on there.

From then on, the world of friend relationships seemed a peculiar thing. At times she would experience great joy and happiness, but most of the time friends pushed her around and she let them. It was as if the creative and optimistic voice she had been born with started to vanish. The one great silver lining was that Teri loved to play the piano and was gifted musically. At a young age, she had worked her way to compete in area Bach competitions and had the privilege of working with a music professor from the University of Santa Barbara. Many days she would come home from school and sit at the piano and play for hours.

Teri had a grandmother who lived in Whittier, California, who was an artist. Her Grandma Sally was very loving and creative, and baked the best pies and cookies Teri had ever eaten. It was always a thrill to visit her and roam through her art studio where she had paints and craft supplies of every imaginable color and texture just sitting out in the open ready to use. One day, Teri was told her grandmother had cancer. She baked less, painted less, and eventually her studio was used no more. The most vivid memory Teri has is when she stood in the garden at the hospital and waved goodbye to her grandmother through the window and she slowly waved back from inside her room for the last time.

For Teri's family, every Sunday was spent at Grandpa Henry's ranch house in Ojai. Orchards of lemons, oranges, and avocados were the playgrounds she and her siblings adventurously explored. Grandpa Henry even let them drive his old Oliver tractor with the big comfy seat and the tricky clutch that made it jerk abruptly forward when it started. He was 100% Italian and loved to cook and entertain. He was very special to Teri. She can still hear him laugh and see the Santa Claus–like twinkle in his eye. When she was told that he, too, had cancer, she was very sad. As his health deteriorated and he was confined to bed, she was asked to play the piano for him. His favorite was Chopin's "Nocturne Op. 9 No. 2." When he died, music didn't interest Teri anymore.

Teri lived with a lot of fear of those dark storm clouds coming back into her life, even when the sky was perfectly clear. Though she didn't understand it then, she struggled on and off with bouts of depression, to the point she wondered at times, why she was even born. She just thought she was crazy. At fifteen, a friend invited her to a local church youth group. It was like nothing she had ever experienced. Teri met Jesus there and asked Him to be the Lord of her life; once again she began to see glimpses of life through eyes of wonder and amazement. She met a kind, young man named James whose family was highly respected in the church. They became good friends and started dating a year later. Life was full of youth group activities, Fellowship of Christian Athletes meetings, leadership groups, and school. It was easy to forget that the dark clouds ever even existed. She began to think that maybe all of the bad stuff wasn't that big of a deal and, possibly, some of it never happened at all.

Fast–forward seven years down the road; James and Teri were happily married and finishing college together. The world was full of exciting possibilities ready to be experienced, but for some strange reason beyond her comprehension, the dark clouds started to come back. Again, she began to think that maybe she was crazy.

She'd be in class or driving down the street and an overwhelming fear would grip her so strong that she felt as if she couldn't breathe. There were even times she would get up from class at the university and run to her car and cry. She was told by well–meaning people at their church to just pray harder. "Why is this happening to me," she thought, "Have I done something wrong?" She stopped talking about it at church when she realized it was anxiety and people told her it was because of fear and she should simply get over it. Teri desperately tried to get over it, but it was so difficult when what she was afraid of was something she couldn't express in words. She allowed it to become a shameful part of who she thought she was, and Teri learned to deal with it quietly on her own.

For the next twelve years, Teri walked on a path that was, at times, riddled with those dark clouds. She and James had been in ministry in one form or another since they graduated college. It would be in this period of time that she would experience the fullness of joy in so many ways, but partake of the deepest pain of tragedy as well. Teri and James were heaven–blessed to have their three beautiful girls during this season of life. It was also in this time period that their unborn twin babies died at four months, Teri had two more miscarriages, and they lost Teri's father to a brain tumor. Teri would often reflect on the true blessings of the amazing things in her life interwoven with such difficult circumstances. It was in these moments that she started to see life's journey differently. She began to trust her Heavenly Father to drive those dark clouds away in an instant, but at the same time, her desire for safety at all costs began to silently suffocate that newfound trust.

The next eight years mark what Teri would describe as the beginning of the end…of the new beginning. Stress and anger were habitual visitors in the Craft home, which was a stark contrast to the happiness, laughter, and joy that was also found there. Everyone, even the children, had crazy schedules that left little to no time to relax or communicate; it was as if everyone was running from something. Ministry began to demand more and more, and the effects on James were becoming evident. Teri focused her attention on everyone else around her, because it was easier not to feel what was going on inside, until one day everything turned upside down, and she was faced with the worst storm she could ever have imagined…

I cried on and off for days after I read this back to myself aloud. Honestly, I hadn't thought about some of these situations for years. *Wow*, I thought, *that's a lot of heartbreak*, and *Wow, God is really full of grace to have helped me through so much, even when I wasn't aware*. Diane helped me, with the guidance of the Lord, to metaphorically, gently run my hand over the scars resulting from the difficult and painful situations in my life. I realized during this exercise that some of those scars were still bleeding. Some of them were in need of care and had been for some time, but I didn't want, or even know how, to go there. That little girl, Teri, was essentially anemic and dying from the inside out.

It is easy when you find yourself in this fragile place to turn your anger toward God, even for a small moment, and ask, "Where were you when all of this was happening?" For me, it felt a little like I had started on the difficult journey that I'd been asked to accept, but now I was the recipient of some really sick joke. I could hear the words of people in my head saying, "God doesn't give you more than you can handle." Honestly, at this point I wanted to shout, "Easy for you to say!" Fortunately, Diane helped me focus my heart back to the goal at hand. "Who is the Teri that God created?" she asked me. "Who did He have in mind when He knit you together in your mother's womb, before all these situations happened in your life?" (Psalm 139:13) Very... long...pause...followed by a tilt of my head and another long pause, punctuated by a lengthy inhale and exhale, as I looked for a moment out the window during one of our sessions. "I don't think I can even accurately answer that," I genuinely replied.

Even though it felt like a pretty pathetic place to be in then, I comprehend now that it was the very best environment for the Lord to speak to my heart regarding His beautiful masterpiece, and, for once, realize He was referring to me. "Teri, the enemy will wound and steal from you in the areas you are most gifted by the Lord," Diane said. "Now you need to go back and ask the Lord to reveal those areas, and redeem and restore what the enemy has stolen." I'm not exaggerating a single bit when I say it took me the entire thirty days until I met with her again to work through this with the relentless help of the Holy Spirit as my guide.

What I uncovered was no less than the most precious and priceless treasure I could have ever been gifted or discovered. It was like I was sitting with my Daddy God, holding the photo album of my life. Together, we reviewed each and every picture, good and bad; He carefully and masterfully revealed the enemy's plan and then covered it with His great love, until those scars were no longer bleeding. The memories were seen through His cross, and my potential in Him began to unfold in an orchestration so sweet and loud, that no fear or pain could subdue its melody.

Here is the plain and simple truth: the enemy had stolen from me all of my life in one way or another, like a big, ugly bully pushing me around. When I realized who I was created to be, that bully was no longer welcome anywhere near me in any capacity. That, of course, doesn't mean he has given up trying to bring me down, it just means I won't be shaken or torn from the ultimate vision of my existence in Christ.

The following are the prophetic promises the Lord revealed to me in this recovery process. I remember these words on a daily basis, as if they are my theme song, and, when necessary, use them as a weapon against a familiar foe who lurks in waiting for me to forget, even for an instant, who I really am.

"Teri Craft, God has created you to be a worshipper, called to boldly and unabashedly proclaim His love and wonder to the hopeless world around you. He has named you a harvester, born to generously give to others with the love of Jesus and reap gently and humbly at His bidding. You have been given a creative and musical gift to share the beauty of a limitless God to those in need of inspiration and to bring joy to the darkest corners of the world." (Psalm 27, Matthew 9:36–38, Psalm 147, Psalm 47.)

It's hard to really understand fully how asphyxiating darkness can be until you are surrounded by it. And whether it is brought on by your own decisions or thrust upon you, it is no less difficult. It reminds me of the scene in *The Fellowship of the Ring* (the first volume of *Lord of the Rings*) when Galadriel bequeaths Frodo with the light of Eärendil and gives him the hopeful benediction, "May it be a light for you in dark places when all other lights go out." He was not given the conventional armament one might have bestowed on a warrior going into battle; instead, he was gifted a strong reminder, an undying light, and a powerful symbol of what they stood for and a hope for their journey that led through very dark places.

I found out firsthand that it's the same with our loving Heavenly Father; though we may not understand the intricacies of His plan for our lives, we can trust that He has given us what we need to navigate, "…when all other lights go out." I remember like it was yesterday, being curled up in a ball on the floor of my bedroom, in the darkest place I think I have ever been in my life. I had been betrayed and we'd lost just about everything. There was nothing left to grasp or hold onto, but the light of God's Word and the bright echoes of His love to the inmost part of my heart. "You're stronger than you know, dear one, you're stronger than you know," was the love song He sang over me.

I now encourage you with the heartfelt authenticity that He gives all of us, that light for the unknown parts of the path we are on, to ultimately guide us to freedom in Him. And though that path may lead through a dark valley that seems like a dead end, lift up your eyes and see that He beckons you toward new life. His all–consuming light is not only there to guide our steps, but also to illuminate the dark places we've closed off inside us, so that we may run this race set before us, unencumbered, and feel the warmth on our face in the high places of victory. (Hebrews 12:1–3)

If you have never written a story of your life in third person similar to the one I wrote, take the opportunity to open your heart to doing it now. When finished, read it aloud to yourself or to someone to whom you are accountable, and let the Lord begin to bring healing to the scars that, like mine, might still be bleeding.

Chapter 6

INTERSECTIONS

*Our humanity intersects with God's sovereignty,
and, if we are open to it, we are forever changed.*

A few years ago, I was in an auto accident at an intersection about a mile from our house. We were on our way to church. It was a beautiful, bright Sunday morning. The sky was clear and blue without a cloud in sight. Two of our girls were with me in the car and we were listening to our favorite, upbeat worship song. Excitement for the day ahead filled our minds. I glanced at the upcoming traffic light and saw green. Here is where it all went wrong. I took my eyes off the approaching intersection and looked at my young daughter in the back seat. In those few seconds the light changed, and our car entered the point of no return. I didn't have enough time to stop before we hit another car. Thankfully, though we were all frightened, everyone was fine.

Fast forward to the summer of 2013, just a few months into our new journey. I was driving to the grocery store and thinking about how much my life had changed. Now, we were back in California and living with relatives; our existence was as far from our norm as we could get. We were making steady progress in our restoration and recovery, but being back in California was bittersweet. This essentially was the epicenter of the pain and betrayal, exposing different layers of needed healing. New pressures surfaced as we were faced with building a new career and seeking the Lord about where our family would fit in to our old surroundings with our new circumstances.

Laughter came back into our family life; tears came when I heard that sweet sound coming from a precious loved one who I know fought hard for its return. These moments became more precious than any monetary gain, and no perceived loss could hold a candle to the purity and sweetness we quietly beheld. This bright, sunny afternoon, I was on my way to the grocery store, and, thankfully, stopped properly at the traffic light and was waiting for my green light to go forward. It's funny, because I'm the first to acknowledge that waiting isn't an easy thing for me to do under most circumstances, especially when three hungry girls are anxious to eat dinner. I quieted my heart for a moment, stopped looking at all the craziness going on around my car, and, in that quick moment, heard the Lord speak to my heart. "Teri, watch for intersections in your life. They will be the primary training and learning ground for your future." *Wow, thank you, God,* I thought to myself, and pretty much plugged on with my errand as if nothing of importance had transpired. I call it busy–mom–mode.

It wasn't until a few days later when we were faced with an issue concerning our eldest daughter that I returned to this moment with the Lord. She is a teenager, and is a beautiful, quietly confident young lady, but we could tell she was straining under a burden. It came out most profoundly with her dad. We confronted her about the short or cold responses we were getting. Her behavior was teetering on disobedience, which was uncommon for her. The bottom line was that she had some real and understandable hurt toward her dad and was unable, and maybe afraid, to speak it, so it came out in angry undertones and cold, heartless replies.

Haven't we all been there? A huge elephant stands in the middle of the room, but no one deals with it, so everyone flings snide, angry remarks around and hopes the elephant will just disappear, all the while inflicting wounds on each other. Well, we have learned that a 10,000 pound elephant is not easy to push out of the room, unless you have the proper tools, technique, and commitment to get the job done. In our case, this is where hard work, the humble love of Christ, and the power of His blood have come in.

When you are breaking a generational pattern of communication, you must be relentless in bringing new experiences to your children, otherwise they will just take whatever is familiar with them into their future. James took our daughter on a walk and opened up his life and heart and, again, authentically repented of any and all actions or behaviors that had caused her pain, either directly or indirectly. She was thankful for the opportunity and then proceeded to give it to him good. She exploded with the disappointment she felt and most profoundly expressed the deep pain she felt that her daddy didn't protect her against the effects of his choices that we were now experiencing. They talked for a long while and dealt with root issues, giving way to freedom for both of them in the healing process.

I listened to them talk about this important conversation later. I was amazed by how Jesus works in our lives when we are open. James was open to humbling himself in repentance and was vulnerable enough to hear her out, no matter what she wanted to say, and our daughter felt safe enough to express what was deep in her heart without fearing reproach. Both of these experiences were new, and the old shame–based way we communicated as a family was being replaced with authentic, vulnerable relationships right before our eyes.

As I reflected later that evening on the events of the afternoon, the Lord reminded me of the words He spoke about intersections in the days prior to this experience. I was listening now, no errands or distractions. "Tell me more about intersections," I said to the Lord. He responded with these words to my heart: "Intersections will be the primary training and learning ground for your future and will give you a heads up for taking an offensive stance against the enemy. Intersections will help you know how you need to fortify against the enemy's new and destructive strategies that are meant to destroy you and your family as you grow in Me." It's a strange thing when the Lord opens your eyes to something so familiar in everyday life, but gives it a new and profound meaning. He was revealing to me that intersections in the spiritual sense are the special place where our humanity intersects with God's sovereignty, and if we are open to it, we are forever changed.

Being the teacher that I am, it was inevitable that I would research intersections and their purpose more fully, both in the spiritual and physical sense. In our most common everyday use, an intersection is the place we come to when driving where we are given the opportunity to do a number of things:

• Wait if the traffic light is red
• Proceed if the traffic light is green
• Slow down when it is yellow
• Choose our direction when roads converge
• Make course adjustments if we are headed in the wrong direction
• Possibly incur or cause injury if we aren't vigilant

I'll be honest, I don't always want to stop, wait, slow down, change direction, or alter my present journey, unless, of course, it's my idea. When we start to recognize intersections in our lives as a means by which God brings us out of captivity, our limited perspective changes. Our temporal existence and circumstances begin to unfold a master plan that is mind blowing.

> *"For I know the plans I have for you," declares the Lord, "plans to prosper you and not to harm you, plans to give you hope and a future. Then you will call on Me and come and pray to Me, and I will listen to you. You will seek Me and find Me when you seek Me with all your heart."*
> Jeremiah 29:11–13

In this beautiful exchange of pain and joy, I began to comprehend that the road to Jeremiah 29:11 leads through some very important intersections in life; when I finally understood that, I could see the sovereignty of God in terms of how much He loves me and is allowing my circumstances to make me a beautiful reflection of Him. It is His desire to take all of us to heights we never thought we could achieve, and help us see, with His eyes, the path before us that leads to life, even if the entire itinerary is temporarily hidden from our view. I admit, I've quoted Jeremiah 29:11 many times in the context of wanting to justify my vision and my plan. When I didn't get my way, I shriveled in sadness thinking my Heavenly Father didn't really love me, when all the while He was orchestrating something beyond my wildest imagination. I often think of the main character played by Ben Stiller in *The Secret Life of Walter Mitty* who, when faced with a crucial situation involving his job as a negative assets handler, plunges into a world of adventure that had only existed in his mind. What he discovers is that he is more courageous than he perceived himself to be, that there is more to life than he ever thought possible, and that he plays a very important role in the lives of those around him. I feel a little like Walter Mitty thrust into something I wasn't planning on, but completely and totally changed by the experience.

I can now approach life's little four-way stops, and even the major interchanges, with a different outlook. Even though my life experiences may not include jumping out of a helicopter, braving an erupting volcano, or climbing a snow-covered mountain peak as Walter did, what awaits me is no less significant. I have found the key to reaching greater heights and experiencing a deeper sense of the "hope and future" of Jeremiah 29:11. That key is found in verses 12 and 13 of that same chapter: "Then you will call on Me and come and pray to Me, and I will listen to you. You will seek Me and find Me when you seek Me with all your heart."

If we find ourselves in intersections of pain, bondage, woundedness, sin, difficult circumstances, confusion, or even great success, the transformation comes when we "call," "pray," "listen," and "seek." I think that's why He starts in verse 11 with the promise. It's like He is saying, "When you find yourself in these places of difficulty, remember I have a good plan for you, but your trust in Me IS the hope and the foundation of the future."

I had to do more than simply understand this. I had to live it out. In my journal I wrote about putting this idea into practice.

JOURNAL ENTRY SEPTEMBER 13, 2013

I woke up this morning after having one of those dreams that feel so real, you have to pinch yourself to make sure you are awake when it is all over. Every once in a while, I have what I would consider, in my unprofessional opinion, a reaction in my soul to the bombshell of hurt and betrayal I suffered months ago. I guess some would call it post–traumatic stress. I woke up from this dream and had a decision to make. Would I stay in this place of hurt, which would lead to bitterness, or would I talk to my Abba Father about it and get His wisdom and council?

Today, I chose the latter. "God, it's hard sometimes to wake up and believe that all those things really happened to me. James and I are discovering a love that is deeper than I ever thought possible, but it's honestly hard to accept sometimes that this is now my story. Help me get better and not bitter. Replace the hurtful pictures in my brain with images of You and me. I know You understand something about betrayal; after all, You hung on a cross on behalf of every one of us in our brokenness. Teach me, Jesus, right now, in this moment, what kept Your focus and what got You through it."

I paused for a second or two, closed my eyes, and heard quietly in my heart, "It was love." That's all I heard, and it was enough. It was as if Jesus was sitting at the foot of my bed, His sweet, loving eyes filling up with tears, looking directly at me with understanding and compassion; with great empathy, my Savior and teacher gave me a gift. He reminded me that He knew firsthand my pain and struggle, that one thing got Him through, and it was the same "one thing" that would get me through, too.

Love. It's a word we toss around flippantly, but I'm coming to a place of realization that it is so much more than just four letters. It's courageous and humble, it's tender and fierce, and it's unconditional and priceless. True love is not obtained easily, but given freely. It's tangible, but elusive, and, above all, a mystery in so many ways to the human heart. Today, and every day, it is my vehicle for living and destination of my purpose here on earth.

So here's where I find myself once again at an intersection with the Lord. Jesus' response to me means I need to apply love to this situation, these thoughts right now, this very instant, before I move an inch in any direction other than His will for me. "Jesus forgive me and replace each of my human reactions with love. Replace any unforgiveness with love, replace any anger with love, replace any envy with love, replace any loneliness with love, replace any doubt with love, and most of all, replace any fear I've allowed in my life with love."

The crazy thing is that my story, my very life, seems okay now, in the light of His love. I know in my heart I share something deep and special with my Jesus, and for all the pain it cost me to get here, His love is and will be enough. Did I ever really know what love was before?

Thank You, my Lord, for teaching me and showing me Your love, Your amazing love.

Though my relationship with the Lord found depth and strength I had not known before, my relationship with the church felt strained. During one of my darker moments early on in this journey, my journal entry for the day was simply this: *August 1, 2013. "I have never felt closer and identified more with the heart of*

God in this grief, and, in the same breath, I've never felt further away from the church." It's very sad to be recovering from trauma, both from the near past and from childhood, as both my husband and I were in our different ways, and to feel isolated from the church. I know that is not what most intended, but realistically, it's what often happens. Add to that our lifetime of ministry involvement, and you get the feeling of sheer abandonment and rejection.

At the beginning, it is understandable, as you are in the ER on life support. A lot of voices are not what you need. However, as the months roll past and you and your family are seeing great miracles of healing and health, and people still stay away, it threatens to jam a wedge between you and the ones who Jesus has called to be His extension of love. What do you do in this situation? As broken followers of Christ, we stood outside the church looking in, trying to make sense of what life and love within the context of the four walls of the church might now look like. It is my heartfelt encouragement to Christ followers who want to see the church grow and expand, both in depth and scope, to put themselves in the shoes of the wrestling, broken soul.

For our family, great sadness threatened to overtake us, and our first thought was to run as fast as we could away from anything that had to do with the organized church. I can't count how many times we called our pastors and said, "We've lost everything. We're walking in genuine repentance and restoration, but we just don't know if we can endure the isolation. It actually seems as if some people want our family to continually suffer." I am so thankful for the loving people who pushed past their judgments, past the awkward feeling of not knowing what to do or say, and extended Christ's hand of mercy and kindness. Our pastors, a handful of friends, and numerous members of our local church body were those people.

To be fair, I believe that most of the time, people just don't know what to do with broken people, so the easy thing to do is just ignore or pretend not to notice them. But I noticed. Our whole family noticed. Even our little ones were confused. You can't really conceal it when people walked right past us as if we were invisible. It is in the context of the church that the greatest amount of healing can come for those straining under the weight of brokenness and, conversely, it can also bring an exponential amount of pain. I understand now, in a greater way, after walking through this process, that we as Christ followers carry a great responsibility as ambassadors, not only to non–believers, but also to the hurting person or family entering the doors of the church in need of His tangible touch.

People have asked me what made us keep coming back when it was so difficult. I can say, without a doubt, it was the grace and love extended to us from our pastors who would say weekly, "We're for the Craft family. You can make it. Don't give up!" Our small group of friends who walked confidently with us and didn't run for the hills when almost everyone else did, and the loving Sunday School teachers who extended the hand of Jesus to our children, making a safe place for them from the storms of hurt they had suffered in the context of ministry. Please understand my heart when I say that if we, as a community, unite with this kind of love and mercy, and are willing to open our eyes to the fact that this issue that affected our family is a real and growing issue, then revelation, knowledge, and grace will be the culture we produce. We need to be intentional. The beauty is that within this intentionality, precious lives will be restored and the Kingdom of God strengthened and expanded.

I know our family isn't the first to have experienced the chasm between those who are healed enough to live out grace and those who say they are healed, but have a hard time functioning in action. As one who knows very well the systems, purpose, and organization of the church as a whole, it began to feel as if my brain was going to pop right open. It's a whole lot different when you're watching this happen to other people. Believe me, as pastors, we orchestrated many whiteboard brainstorming activities about this very thing. But it gets painfully real when it hits you in the face. "What's the point of it all?" I began to think. Then a light bulb went on in my head.

Teri, this is what so many of the young adults you've ministered to would say. This is what the teens and college age students would sit in your office complaining about for hours; you used to try your hardest to understand, but just didn't. Well, now I did. And like that day I was given a choice to either run or stay in the battle for my marriage and family. We now, as a motley little crew, had to choose, choose whether to forgive as Christ forgave. This is what we discovered…

JOURNAL ENTRY OCTOBER 1, 2013

We are never closer to the heart of Jesus and identifying with Him more than when we press in toward true forgiveness motivated by love. There is a release and an impartation in this posture that is supernatural and divine. It's as if God Himself allows us into the deepest place of His existence—the place that springs with the kind of love that drove Him to the cross, and the resurrection power that makes all things, including our fragile lives, new!

The victim becomes the heavenly victor. It is then that we are free and truly have hope of being changed, and can bring change to the people around us. The pure love of Christ is unhindered by our humanity, and He is seen once again on this earth."

This is the stuff that life–changing intersections are made of, and is primarily what non–believers and the next generation are looking for in all of us as we navigate our very visible journey in their presence. The following is a post I saw on a social media site from a young adult in her early twenties, who happens to be an incredible young woman of God. She expresses something I've heard over and over in my life. Not until now did I really relate. Not until now do I empathize, genuinely have ears to hear, and honestly mean to do something discernible about it.

If we disregard the homeless, the strippers, the drug addicts, the alcoholics, the special needs, the pop stars, the actors/actresses, the homosexuals, those addicted to pornography, the adulterers, the victims AND the offenders…we are disregarding the entire message God called us to give. Let's get out of our comfort zones and spread His LOVE…to EVERYONE.[8]

It is with a heart bursting with the love and grace Jesus revealed to me in this crazy, new journey that I say to Carley and every child, tween, teen, twenty–something, college student, and young married, "I'm sorry." *I'm so deeply sorry that I, and so many others like me, haven't always lived this out in the way Jesus demonstrated for us. I'm sorry because it has taken me this much time, and this much pain, to truly hear what you've been saying all these years.*

It's been in this tragic and beautiful intersection that I've come to realize, that I chose on whom to bestow grace, as if it was my choice to begin with. Even if I didn't say it out loud, I spoke it with my actions; the older I got, and the deeper my issues became, the further away from real, grace–filled empathy

---

[8] Carley Redpath (personal communication, November 23, 2013)

I got. I let fear and the busyness of life conveniently distract me from truly being about my Father's business. Busyness and "the program" I had down; His heart and His love, I regret to say, not so much. With all my heart, I'm sorry.

Do you know how humbling it is to admit that for the twenty years I ministered in one way or another in the church, I didn't properly grasp the love of Jesus for His beloved? You know, the ones He said He came for—the broken, the hurting, and the harassed? The ones Carley described in her message. I didn't know this kind of love, because I was too afraid to go there. I was too afraid to go deep down into the places of my heart that were wounded because that would mean I had to feel those pains deeply in my own personal life in order to feel deeply for others.

Dear friend, I know you may have a lot of different thoughts and emotions clanging around in your head as you read this, but may I encourage you? Please consider taking the time to pray and ask the Lord to review the intersections of your life, the places that, for one reason or another, you, like me, may have picked up a burden or allowed unforgiveness to become bitterness. A circumstance occurred and grace may have been replaced with a cold, judgmental thought process. Let the Holy Spirit bring to mind wounds and past hurts that you can start to deal with. Through His love and power, you can reclaim your heart, the heart that can bring healing to others.

Never in a million years would I have thought it would be my story that would ring of such brokenness, the kind of brokenness that comes from the effects of abuse, addiction, deception, and betrayal. But the fact remains, it is my story; I have one path that leads to life, and that is the road that is walked in close proximity to the Lord. Through His great love for me, my Heavenly Father has led me through intersections and will continue to do so until the day I die. It is what comes out of those intersections and experiences that will either change my life and others around me for eternity, or get me stuck in a pothole and invariably cause someone else to stumble or crash.

You could say this last season of my life has been one huge, life-changing intersection. Though difficult, I am in awe of the all-consuming love and peace my Heavenly Father has wrapped around me and our family. I understand now that the places my life intersects with change, whether that change seems good or bad on the surface, is a place of divine training and purpose-filled preparation meant to mold my heart and life for the glory of God. If I am watching and listening, I just might change the world around me, too.

You may feel isolated and estranged from the church at this point in your life. I know that it is one of the hardest places to be. You long to fit in and have someone embrace you in your time of need; at the same time, you guard your life and keep one foot out the front door because you are afraid to get hurt worse. I don't profess to have all the answers, but I do know that even though there are many flaws in the human existence here on earth, the church is still the Bride for whom Christ died. It took me a year of choosing to push in and move beyond the pain, shame, and unforgiveness that was keeping me distanced from the church. I realize now that I am called to be the change I want to see happen around me, and that change happens most profoundly in relationship and fellowship with those who, like me, are walking one day at a time with Jesus, our only hope.

Chapter 7
DON'T LOSE HEART

You can never learn that Christ is all you need,
until Christ is all you have.

Corrie Ten Boom[9]

I grew up with brothers and married a very athletic man. I've been privy to more football games than I care to recall. I reluctantly admit, I've truly taken an interest in watching football with my family. What brings me the most joy is the great comeback story: a team is losing badly, all hope seems lost, they arrive back on the field after halftime, and they fight their way to victory. I've always wondered what was said in the locker room that turned the tide. What words were used to bring motivation and focus to the goal at hand? All I know is when the team pushes past the line of impending defeat and triumphs, it's something unforgettable!

You may be wondering why I'm contemplating the benefits of a good halftime motivational speech at this point in my story. Well, here it goes. I discovered a very important truth on this journey of recovery—there is only one thing harder than starting, and that's the halfway mark. About the time the leaves started

---

9   Corrie Ten Boom quoted in Joseph Gillespie, *Trusting Relationships* (WestBow Press, August 2012).

changing color and our family looked down the road to the upcoming holiday season, much of life had radically changed.

James had been walking in freedom from his former addiction for some time, we were experiencing a newfound joy that came from a vulnerable and transparent relationship, and our family was learning daily how to communicate without fear and anger, but our outward circumstances were still up in the air, a few hundred feet above our heads spinning around like debris from an F5 tornado.

Do you know how hard it is to keep coming up to the line when you have spent countless hours a day, for half a year, putting every ounce of strength into your marriage and family restoration and you barely have enough money to live on? We were faced with having to put our faith in God for every single area of our lives. We didn't get to keep any convenient go-tos. Looking back on the situation, I can see that it was the best thing for us.

Of course, this is one of those observations you recognize in hindsight, but struggle through in real time. We made the choice early in our process to put everything we had into recovery for the sake of our marriage and our kids. In doing so, we said "no" to career directions that might be a hindrance to that end, namely situations that would put us both back into a stress-filled, hectic pace, apart from our family and our recovery. But as many can attest, the right decisions can often be the hardest to walk out.

We chose to put our entrepreneurial gifts to the test and work together to build a business from the ground up with the help of a generous and kind man of God who believed in us. Talk about an exercise in faith for everyone involved! As you may remember, my fleshly default is to seek safety at all costs. Does this sound like one of those safe situations? Not even close! I found myself waking up each day having to expend such a great deal of my energy just to keep my focus for normal day–to–day functioning that I became extremely weary in the process.

What was really happening was that we were approaching another important intersection where God was helping us discover that He is our provider and our sustainer—not man, not our efforts or giftedness, but God, and God alone. We had always believed this to be true, but, candidly, belief is put to the test when you are stretched for months with no relief and you must choose and choose again to actually live what you say you believe. As a family, we got very acquainted with the concept of manna (Exodus 16). Can I just say that manna can taste as good as a hot fudge sundae with a cherry on top when it comes just in the nick of time? It's really all about perspective, and we were being taken through a God–sized boot camp regarding faith, peace, and the concept of directional provision. Here's a little glimpse into how I was dealing with the situation in that moment.

JOURNAL ENTRY NOVEMBER 14, 2013

Dear God,

Today I find myself feeling overwhelmed by our circumstances. As I sit at the park watching a young mom play with her toddler, I ache inside trying to remember those intimate moments with my girls years ago. How did time fly by so fast? How could I have known that this life would have led me here to this place of desperation? So many new and good experiences have entered into our lives and home, but I feel as if we are one step from the curb and living on the streets.

Lord, I am scared, and I can't fix this. The last thing either James or I want to do is make some kind of knee–jerk decision to get temporary relief and throw us off the course of Your ultimate plan. Please, show Yourself strong on our behalf. I want to believe that I can do all things through You, but I'm having a hard time walking it out.

I slowly meandered home that day past the familiar homes that dotted the walking path. I wondered if any of the families living in those structures were struggling like we were struggling. Is there anyone who understands? Just then my mind thought of a Corrie Ten Boom quote I'd read many times, but didn't relate to until now. "You can never learn that Christ is all you need, until Christ is all you have"[10] I was being reminded by this beautiful example that when we face adversity in a posture of humility, Christ can do His finest work. It is so true that sometimes, all it takes is a few words to change your perspective entirely. After all, isn't that what a good halftime speech does for us when we are down and out, and ready to call it quits? It helps us see beyond the moment and propels us to take another step toward the goal.

I'm truly glad that "Jesus Christ is the same yesterday, today and forever" (Hebrews 13:8), and that He will use whatever is available in our surroundings to impart what we specifically need in terms of motivation for our journey. That quote became my mantra helping me focus my attention where it needed to be… NOT on my circumstances and myself.

I wish I could say it all got better in one week, but the fact is, we still struggled in our finances for some time. I suppose I shouldn't have been surprised. We were starting from ground zero in almost every aspect of our lives. For a long stretch of time, we made it through each month having to pay out more than we brought in, and somehow it all balanced out. There was no safety net or extra stash for emergencies, but somehow there

---

10   Corrie Ten Boom quoted in Joseph Gillespie, *Trusting Relationships* (WestBow Press, August 2012).

was enough for the essentials. I had to put on the chopping block my preconceived notions of what I thought life should look like and how much I needed to have in my checking account to feel safe, especially during the approaching Christmas season.

God, in His sovereign orchestration, was working on us from the inside out, but it was clashing with my outward expectations. The crazy thing is, our circumstances not only didn't get better, they got worse. If you can believe it, we got robbed of every last dime in our checking account just a few days before Christmas due to internet fraud. It is some very profound truth that the Lord takes what the enemy has meant for destruction and turns it for good. You see, He didn't change the situation, but He changed our hearts in it. In the long run, that's what we pray for anyway, right?

JOURNAL ENTRY DECEMBER 20, 2013

Being in ministry in one way or another for twenty years, Christmas had become a destination instead of a starting point for me. Christmas was comprised of planning, practicing, pushing, decorating, organizing, and orchestrating. And, of course, I would not be happy unless excessive shopping, wrapping, and baking were thrown in the mix as well. Christmas 2013 has turned out completely different from what my heart has grown to expect.

As a family, we experienced a holiday season with not one high–pressure engagement on the books. Where hundreds of cards would find their way into our mailbox in the past, now just a few special notes of kindness trickled in. We had no big parties to attend and no productions to lead. Now, with no money in the bank, we'd been left with a very important decision to make. It was like my personal identity had attached itself to the busyness of the season. That nonsense came to an immediate and abrupt halt. This was truly a different kind of Christmas. It was different at first because I felt isolated and alone. I watched people hustle and bustle as if they had somewhere important to be and I didn't get the memo. I felt a little like the lost kid in the crowded mall searching for someone who would claim her. What I found when I quieted my heart was much more profound.

As I pressed into the Lord's leading, I discovered a facet of our precious Savior I had not touched on before in my self–sustaining holiday frolic. Our fragile family looked at each other huddled around the Christmas tree, knowing that we were momentarily estranged and penniless; miraculously, something in our hearts changed. Christmas became the manifestation of grace and unconditional love personified. In our broken and uncomfortable state, we touched the stuff of heaven.

It wasn't a loud and boisterous declaration, but more a quiet revelation that happened in the still of the night, a very reminiscent echo of our Savior's birth those many years ago. "This is why He came," and "Jesus is the reason we celebrate in the first place," were words that rolled off our lips as we got a real life lesson from Emmanuel, "God with us." And like those lonely and outcast shepherds that special night two thousand years ago, we were invited to see the wonder of God. The multi–billion dollar holiday machine that we had contributed to for years got simplistic and personal. Jesus came knocking, and we were quiet enough to listen and respond.

It's truly amazing when the Lord does something that changes your overall perspective in a way you would least expect or even desire. It's very difficult to explain in words what transpires in these moments, other than to divulge the truth that it is as close to a divine recalibrating back to the Creator's original settings as one can get. If it is true that God created our inmost being and knit each and every one of us together in our mother's womb, then it is safe to say He can be trusted when a reboot is necessary (Psalm 139). That's what essentially happened to me in the quiet of that Christmas evening; on the outside it may have looked as if I was on the losing team, but, in fact, I was poised to see the motivation behind the greatest comeback story ever told.

My mind drifts back to one of my long walks along Waimanalo Beach in Hawaii in May 2013. Amidst the worst time in my life, I uttered under my breath, "Lord, I have never experienced You in such a magnificent way in my entire existence. I will give up anything in this life that separates me from You now that I have tasted the sweetness of Your presence in such a beautiful way." It's funny to think that in just half a year's time, I had already put my fear and desire for things ahead of the One who had shown me, in inexplicable ways, how steadfast and faithful was He. How quickly I reverted back to my personal preset of wandering in the desert of despair that November day when I wrote that journal entry questioning if we were going to end up on the streets. It took some retraining and renewing of my mind, but I eventually got the rhythm of what the Lord was showing me.

JOURNAL ENTRY JANUARY 23, 2014

Philippians 4:13
"I can do all things through Christ who strengthens me."

I'm realizing to a greater degree that Philippians 4:13 is a reality, a reality in a more powerful and all–encompassing way than I previously was aware of. I understand now how with bold and loving confidence, Paul wrote, "I can do all things through Christ who gives me strength." This heartfelt confession came out of the honest account of his journey through life's circumstances and the faithful God who met him at his greatest points of need. This is a man who gets it! This grace–filled, once wretched unbeliever, overcoming sinner, beaten and abused man of God, who experienced both good and bad, fullness and hunger, wealth and poverty, understood from the top of his head to the bottom of his feet, that there is NOTHING that he and Jesus couldn't make it through together (Philippians 4:11–13).

I'm guilty of tossing this verse around at will, and it became the go–to phrase I pulled out when I needed to see something done in my life, which isn't always a bad thing. What I understand now through my life experience and the context in which Paul is writing, however, is that in reality it looks a whole lot more like Paul and me sitting side–by–side in a dark, dingy, dirty jail cell with my life and faith on the line. Not all the answers have come, and I'm holding as tightly as I possibly can to Jesus.

To my surprise, something that feels like joy leaps out of me, and I turn to my fellow prisoner, Paul, and say, "I get it now, too, Paul. I get it now. No matter my circumstances, and I've had a lot of amazingly good things come my way, but now in this dark and difficult place I can laugh, and maybe cry. I can even sing a worship tune or two, and I'm not scared or afraid. I have a calm I've never been able to produce on my own. And Paul, I'm so very excited to encourage those around me after I'm released from this place. You see, I think…no, I KNOW…they will see from my life's testimony that there is truly NOTHING, no situation or crisis that can be thrown their way, that they cannot be content in, and ultimately overcome, through the strength of Jesus Christ."

I REALLY dislike dirty, dark, smelly places like the jail cell described above. And for the most part, I run as fast as I can from anything that looks like hardship, confrontation, or adversity. So why, for the love of all that is good, would I willingly identify with that scenario? Why would I say that joy is present when I am in that place? The truth is, everyone, at one time or another, finds themselves in the storms of life that come, whether or not they appear on Doppler Radar. And when they come, if we're open to it, we are given something very sacred and special by our Savior that nothing of this earth can hold a candle to.

I have never considered myself to be anywhere close to the same league as Paul. I have often read the Scriptures and placed an unhealthy awe on the people described in those pages. The bare fact remains that Paul was given a free will to make each and every situation in his life either point up or point down, and so have we, period. Why, then, do I sometimes live in shame thinking that I will never attain the kind of relationship Paul had with the Lord?

I understand now that our commonality doesn't just come from reading the Word and identifying with a specific person's situation, but it also comes from the fact that we are given the same opportunities that Paul was, to live in response to our Father. Our common ground then becomes the space between Paul and the Lord, that supernatural place where miracles can and do take place, where we are embraced by our Father in such a way that words can't describe, where we discover and accept the message of Romans 8 "that if we are led by the Spirit of God, we are called His children." That though we may suffer, we have hope that we will also be glorified in Him and through Him. That what will unfold when we put our faith in Jesus is simply unimaginable, no matter what we think He has to work with.

What I am trying to make clear is something I am learning more and more each day on this new journey. When we find ourselves in need of a halftime motivational speech, coaxing us not to give up, it is very important to make sure that we are fighting for the right goal. "Things" won't ultimately make us happy, even if we have very little. What if I fought hard and gained all the "things" in the whole world, but lost my connection with the One who formed my heart? I'd feel empty, discouraged, and desperate, and be no good to anyone. I would thirst and never be satisfied. I don't want to live that way, and I pray you don't either.

I am reminded of Moses' response to the Lord in Exodus 33:15–16 (NLT). He vulnerably says to the Lord, "If You don't personally go with us, don't make us leave this place. How will anyone know that You look favorably on me—on me and on Your people—if You don't go with us? For Your presence among us sets Your people and me apart from all other people on the earth." In other words, Moses was contending with the Lord for their victory, both personally and corporately. This kind of victory goes deeper than crossing a river, or acquiring land; he was contending for the whole enchilada. The kind of relationship Moses experienced along the road of suffering when the Lord met him with a supernatural and personal touch, was spiritually, emotionally, and even physically changing. That is a victory worth fighting for, and Moses knew they would not live a life of freedom apart from God's presence. The same goes for us in the present day.

I pray this resonates in your heart the way it has with mine. The Lord has so patiently and lovingly walked with me on this journey, showing me that I'm ineffectual in my life, and in the lives of those around me, if I am willing to fight for a goal that will ultimately lead to emptiness and destruction—even if it seems good on the outside. Dear friend, it should be our life's goal to be in one accord with the Lord in a way that every other aspect of life just flows out of that wellspring. I have gotten to the point, on a good day mind you, that I can say, that though I would never have chosen this difficult path, I am glad for what my Abba Father is producing because of it.

You may feel as if you have crawled into the locker room after battling like mad for the first half has gotten you nowhere fast. In a sweat–dripping–down–your–forehead, grass–stained–jersey, and every–muscle–in–your–body–aching kind of way, I get it. But don't lose heart, halftime is just that: halftime. While the bling–bling show, featuring some special guest like Katy Perry, is taking place on the field with all the flashing lights, you and I have the opportunity to kick back, rest a moment, reflect, contemplate, and hear the words of our Heavenly Coach, "Be strong and courageous, do not be afraid or terrified because of them, for the Lord your God goes with you; He will never leave you or forsake you" (Deuteronomy 31:6). You see, sometimes obedience is the sacrifice, well, the *momentary* sacrifice, that leads to the place of ultimate victory in Jesus Christ, and that victory is being close to Jesus Christ.

Chapter 8
FROM BONDAGE
TO BLESSINGS

Pioneer...

You will be extraordinary,
The tree our roots have grown.
You will sow what we have planted,
and know what we have known.[11]

Jonathan Thulin

The words of this song, written and composed by our friend Jonathan Thulin, are a poignant reminder to all of us of the very relevant and significant role we play in future generations. The question I have learned to ask myself is, "What would our tree look like if it grew up right in our front yard and produced a harvest out of the deep roots that no one could see?"

We now understand very deeply that it is our obligation to be responsible for those who are watching us, who will first learn of their Heavenly Father through our modeling, and who desperately want real and authentic grace–filled love to be their foundation. The Lord has entrusted those who are pioneering a

---

11 Jonathan Thulin, *Pioneer* from *The Anatomy of a Heartflow*, Dream Records. 2012, compact disc.

path to do it in such a way that will set His precious lambs on a path to lifelong freedom. What does it mean to lay a foundation for our children or those we lead that sets them on a path as far away from bondage as we humanly can manage and into blessings? I've learned that it starts with me.

It starts with my understanding of who I am in Christ and being open and honest enough to deal with the hard stuff that gets in the way of that knowledge (2 Corinthians 10:4–5). James has come to that same revelation, and together we have seen the Lord create newness in our lives that will translate into health for our children. I understand, with all that is in me, that the best decision I can make for my children and their children to come, is to get free in Christ, thereby unleashing a pathway unhindered and unencumbered by the wounds that drove my behavior, regardless of if those actions were subtle in nature or glaringly obvious.

I've taught piano lessons for close to twenty years. It's one of my favorite things to spend my time doing. I love to see a student work hard practicing a piece of music and just nail it! I have to admit, however, that I am not a perfect piano teacher. I have a bad piano habit of allowing my pinky finger to stick straight up when I play and I don't even notice it half the time.

When my eldest daughter was very young I started to teach her how to play. We'd sit at the piano with my hand over hers as we played each note together. As she progressed and began to play a few easy songs on her own, I noticed her itty–bitty, pinky finger sticking straight up as she played. "Why are you doing that, Rachel?" I asked. "Where did you learn that?" I can still picture her cute, innocent face looking back at me as she shrugged her shoulders. How did I think she wouldn't pick that one up? We sat together every time she practiced and my bad piano habit became hers. Did she mean for that to happen? Absolutely not.

It was her keenest desire to please me, but I was teaching her incorrectly. It was never my intention to teach her improperly, but I hadn't taken the time to recondition my finger to the proper technique. I realize this is just a small example, but the concept is the same if multiplied by time, life circumstances, spiritual freedom or bondage, and behavioral patterns unknowingly transferred from one precious life onto another.

I look back at our time of recovery and the continuing restoration process and realize that God is, and was, orchestrating a masterpiece of generational proportion. You may recall that my husband and I had spent most of our ministry experience working with or advocating for the next generation. We'd held national conferences and employed phenomenal speakers to motivate students all over the world. We'd collaborated with and convened leaders from all denominations to bring awareness to the call of reaching youth in need of hope. But, by far the best and most lasting decision we've ever made as a couple in regard to the next generation, is that of exposing the bondage deep in our family system and fighting hard with the help of the Lord to seek healing. I am not saying that any of our previous endeavors were unfruitful, but I am saying the potential for meaningful impact is immeasurable if each and every believer would live out freedom and grace that give our youth a real and fighting chance in a world that is coming at them from all directions. The principle is that we teach what we believe to be true deep down inside whether we are aware of it or not; no matter how much Scripture we layer over it or words we say to the contrary, the next generation is going to emulate the authentic, good or bad.

Frequently, I am asked to describe what I've learned in this process that would be helpful for others either dealing with the same issue or for those wanting to steer clear of its destruction. The only way I can communicate it is not so much a list of dos or don'ts, but, rather, discoveries that have served as signposts along the uphill road to victory. They are hard–won truths and principles that we will live out for the rest of our lives. I hope they will be an inspiration to you of the indescribable opportunity you have to leave a beautiful and lasting legacy that will point wholly to Christ.

SIGNPOSTS ON THE ROAD TO VICTORY
(In no particular order)

Nothing brings healing and harmony like truth and vulnerability. After James had been delivered from the veil of deception in his life, walls broke that had been built between us, allowing for a safe environment for me to ever so slowly begin to trust again. When our children began to see daddy and mommy living vulnerably and honestly, dealing with the good and bad, in the light of God's love, they, too, stepped out and began to feel secure in communicating their own issues of fear, hurt, or mistrust. Empathy entered our home and imparted a sweet smelling aroma of the heart of our Lord. After all, what is more vulnerable than Jesus praying in the garden or hanging on the cross? If our Savior, who put Himself in our shoes and bore our deepest pains and sin, can be that vulnerable and honest, then we know we're not alone (Hebrews 4:15). Truth and vulnerability were, and will continue to be, the basis of the freedom we enjoy and the vehicle to see that freedom continue for our lifetime and for those who follow behind.

We didn't travel alone. Though our accountability group was a small number of trusted individuals, they were a very sacred part of our process. Without them, we would have crashed and burned. To those individuals I say, "Thank you. You know who you are, because you helped us pack and move more than once, you sent grocery gift cards when we were in need, and you wiped away tears. You took an offering for a broken family when you didn't have to, and you loved us and waited patiently and optimistically to see God heal and restore, before you even knew if we were going to make it or not. You realized that you needed healing from your past in order to respond to us like Christ would. You helped with resume writing and gave us job opportunities that we were not yet qualified for, but hung on and watched as the Lord expanded our skill set. You loved our girls when so many just said goodbye. You asked the "why" questions and didn't let us run when things got messy. You sent encouraging text messages right when we needed them, and you prayed and didn't give up on us. You saw beyond your sadness or anger and loved us like Jesus would. We will forever be grateful."

We learned more from grace than we ever did through judgment and shame. Our family mindset is now, "When in doubt, give 'em grace." In a desire to dissuade ourselves and others from anything that looks and tastes like failure, it is easy to unintentionally shame someone, but our family now deeply understands the need for grace in life's darkest moments. Grace given by others actually propelled us forward and closer to our Heavenly Father, more than any other action or communication delivered in the contrary heart. I am not justifying failure or condoning sinful behavior, but rather reiterating the heart of Paul when he communicated in Romans 2:4 (NLT), "Don't you see how wonderfully kind, tolerant, and patient God is with you? Does this mean nothing to you? Can't you see that His kindness is intended to turn you from your sin?"

We will not compromise on our family values. Early on in our process, Dr. Ted told us that the most effective form of recovery and restoration is done as a family unit so that family systems issues can be addressed. This essentially means that the issue affected everyone, so everyone needed to be healed and redirected toward healthy living. One aspect we enjoyed greatly was establishing our Craft Family Values. We all sat around the dinner table, our new favorite hangout spot, and contributed to these important values—values that we as a family would not compromise, to the very best of our ability. We would be committed to helping one another when needed along the way. It was so much fun watching everyone collaborate and create the framework of what was important to each of us individually. To this day, these values hang framed in our living room as a reminder because there are days we all need a reminder! In case you are wondering, here are our values: Obedience, peacemaking, fun, athletics, unconditional love, joy, honesty, self–control, love of God, respect, kindness, trustworthiness, and responsibility.

God is sovereign and can be trusted even when it doesn't make sense. Whenever we tell our story, I boldly proclaim, "God is who He says He is." You don't have to go very far in the Word of God to discover that He is pretty awesome! Now the real test is this: do you believe it to be true in relation to your life, even when things are completely turned upside down, or when the journey ahead seems pretty impossible, do you know–that–you–know that God's got this? Ponder this:

"For my thoughts are not your thoughts, neither are your ways my ways," declares the Lord. "As the heavens are higher than the earth, so are My ways higher than your ways and My thoughts higher than your thoughts."
Isaiah 55:8–9

Aren't you glad that God has a bird's eye view of our most difficult situations, and is in the eternal business of steering us heavenward? I know life can get discouraging, but don't lose heart, dear friend, because as we discovered, God really does have you and will keep you in His perfect peace if you trust in Him (Isaiah 26:3).

You can have lots of family fun on a very tight budget. When you pull up your bank account on the computer and what you see is dismal, to say the least, what do you do with three active children? We decided to make the very most of our circumstance by creating ways to bond as a family, even if we didn't have lots of money to go out to the movies, eat at restaurants, visit theme parks, or stay in hotels. Guess what? Those crazy days will undoubtedly be some of the best memories of our lifetime. We pulled out the board games, went for bike rides, played the soundtrack from Disney's *Frozen* over and over while choreographing roller skating routines, and made lots of homemade meals from whatever was in the refrigerator and pantry. We frequently drove to the free parking area at Zuma Beach in Malibu with our surfboards and Carpentaria State Beach with our paddle boards, or walked the mall perfecting our "window shopping." You could find us regularly hiking the trails near our home and swimming at the neighborhood pool. We were all together and it was pretty cool, so cool, in fact, that some of those listed activities are what we do weekly to this day. Our youngest daughter Grace, whom we affectionately call our "Mother Teresa," almost always ends one of these low budget, family fun days by saying, "This was the best day of my life!" Enough said.

You must make time in your schedule to hear God. We now realize as parents that we CAN control the pace of our home. No one can make us run around frantically, day after day, if we choose not to. Hear me carefully when I say that it's not God's plan for you either. I would also add that if you are struggling in this area, please take a deeper look at your life and ask why you are running at such a breakneck speed; you can also bring someone into your process to help create margins. If we are children of God, we need to take the time to hear His voice; if we don't, then how in the world is the world going to see His imprint on our lives and desire that same hope and peace? Sometimes, pausing to allow the Lord to touch our lives comes in moment by moment adjustments.

A good example of this was our very interesting Mother's Day 2014. By interesting, I mean it was one of the best days we've shared with each other and the Lord in the whole year, but it didn't start out that way. The morning was a bustle of preparation to get our outfits and hair just right, after all we were taking family pictures at church that morning. I'm not sure what caused the shift, but all of a sudden it turned into a combat zone in our bathroom, and everyone started arguing. I became a referee while at the same time dodging flying hair ties and scraping beauty products off the floor and ceiling. Needless to say, I was getting frustrated. I had pictured one of those carefree mornings. It was Mother's Day, right? My perfect day felt like it was ruined. James herded the kids in the car. We were now five minutes late, but, by golly, we were going to church.

As if a light turned on in my head, I had a thought, "You can change the pace here, Teri. What's really important, attending a service or resolving this tension?" So I sat down on the end of my bed and waited. James came back in the house first and asked, "Are you okay?" "Well…no," I told him. "We all need to talk." The five of us sat at the table and talked for almost forty-five minutes. There was laughing, crying, and apologizing followed by forgiving, hugging, and a family prayer. Afterward, we stopped at a local bakery and uncharacteristically loaded up on carbs and headed to the beach with our extended family in the afternoon.

It's hard to describe, but something wonderful broke free that day in every one of our relationships and the catalyst was stopping and allowing the Lord to work. Taking the time to express issues that were causing tension released the Holy Spirit to heal the little cracks of hurt and offense that can easily creep into any family situation. We essentially had our own, private church service there in the intimacy of our home, followed by living out the peace and joy God had deposited in our hearts that morning. We shared it with everyone we came in contact with the rest of the day. Did I ever get my Mother's Day picture? No, but what I got was something far greater.

Speak blessings over your children and loved ones every day. If the Word of God tells us "the tongue has the power of life and death" (Proverbs 18:21), then it is safe to say that our mission, if we choose to accept it, is to breathe life into the hearts and minds of the ones God has entrusted to us daily. I see it less like a ritual these days and more like a deliberate, Holy Spirit–driven paint stroke on the beautiful masterpiece God is making of my loved ones' lives. It's a big deal to guide and encourage anyone, especially my children, and I believe it's one of the very reasons I exist. As James and I went through the process of hearing the Lord for the promises in our lives; we did the same for our children, making a commitment to speak these promises directly to them daily. The beauty of it is that is comes back around.

The following is a message our middle daughter, Elise, who was eleven years old at the time, inscribed on the front page of one of our recovery workbooks. "I love you, Mom and Dad. I know God is doing the best in you; I can see it. You have made it through this and that means it is one step closer to a new journey." She signed it both by printing her name and signing it as if to say, *I mean this!* She didn't tell us what she had done, but rather waited for us to find it, and find it we did...on one of those days we really needed the encouragement. *Thank you, Elise, for reminding us of who we are and what we are called to do!*

We said goodbye to shame–based language and negative sarcasm. As I alluded to previously in the book, we had to relearn communication patterns as we navigated toward health. This was one of the most impactful changes we made, bringing peace and safety to our marriage and children. Communication patterns can be very subtle, so the process of relearning them was very difficult. The bottom line is that when you use any language that disparages or denigrates in order to get your point across, or you push or maneuver to feel in control or satisfied but cause the other person to feel hurt—even if it is joking, then you are most likely using shame–based communication. This runs side by side with the level of empathy found in the home. If you *don't* empathize, or put yourself in the place of another, then you have no problem saying whatever rolls off the top of your tongue. When we started to notice what this shame–based language sounded like, we were amazed at how frequently people, ourselves included, communicated in this fashion.

THE SIGNPOSTS THAT MARKED OUR WAY

I reflect back on the life–changing moment when I walked back to our townhouse on April 25, 2013, and heard the Lord quietly whisper to my broken heart, "Pursue, and all will be recovered." At the time, I naively longed for the Lord to restore my old life, not realizing that we had found our identity in a misguided, performance–based and shame–based mindset with actions that followed suit. For clarification, when I refer to wanting our "old life," I'm making reference to the fact that I was initially inclined to desire all the perceived "safety" of position and financial stability, and accept the woundedness and dysfunction along with it. I wanted the "B" version of God's best for us in terms of our internal health; at that moment, I was willing to take the "B" version in order to make everything instantly okay.

What we came to realize through intense dedication and reliance on God as we bailed water out of our cracked, compromised, and quickly sinking ship, was that we really didn't want the old people we were, rather, we wanted what God intended when He created us, before all the brokenness had wreaked havoc on our lives. What does that look like? To be quite honest, it's not all laid out before us yet. Remember those healing circles? We are on a journey indeed, but we are loving each day in the Lord, with our identity firmly fitted in the palm of His hand, free and clear of the asphyxiating bondage that held our family down for too long.

CHAPTER 8 – FROM BONDAGE TO BLESSINGS

I watch my husband breathe deeply the fresh, life–giving air of freedom and liberty in Christ, and I don't even recognize him as the same man he once was. He is still one of the best communicators I have ever heard, but he now communicates in a way that is pure, honest, and vulnerable. And I have found my voice. I see myself as an optimistic, creative, and fierce worshipper made by God to love on the world around me, and I'm ready for action. Our girls are learning to walk vulnerably and authentically with God and their parents. It is our greatest hope and prayer that they will take hold of all their loving Father created them to be and do. Other than that, it is like we're holding a blank, white page. We have the wind–in–our–sails, cleared–for–takeoff kind of contentment that Jesus has this well in hand and He'll make our lives what He wants them to be— imperfections and all.

Now, dear reader, I invite you to come closer one last time. Come sit by my side and read the letter I hold in my hands. These are words intended for my husband, but I share them with you as well, because I know your heart may be tired and you need a friend who has walked this path before you. Know that I am imperfect, but that our Father's love for us is not. I pray that though you may feel overwhelmed by the darkness and despair, that you will "… grope for Him and find Him, though He is not far from each of us" (Acts 17:27). He stands faithfully by your side.

Seek and you will find
Matthew 7:7

Dear James,

As my fingers type this, I will have known you 27 of my 42 years of life, and we just celebrated 22 years of marriage this past July 2014. I could have never imagined the twists and turns that have marked our path as we've journeyed heavenward. I beam with an un‑fabricated smile that is the result of the love and joy residing deep in my heart. You are an overcomer, my dearest love. You and I and our girls are overcomers. I suppose as believers in the risen Lord, we shouldn't be surprised. It was His grace and power, motivated by His crazy, amazing love that not only laid the foundation for our freedom, but also gave us the super‑powered fuel we needed for this difficult journey. I love you more today than I ever thought possible. What we share is simply a unique and divine glimpse into the heart of God for His creation. You are courageous and kind, loving and selfless, devoted and honest. You are daily becoming the James God had in mind when He created you. I watched you for 365 days straight devote hours upon hours to recovery, transformation, and restoration, and for 365 days you showed up, letting your Heavenly Father and your accountability partners work something new and authentic in your life.

Graciously you loved as people dumped their entire life's hurt at your feet and called it yours. I saw you choose and choose again to do the right thing, which was almost always the hardest thing.

It is my deepest joy to watch you interact with our girls and know that kind of love cannot be counterfeited. I've seen you laugh, cry, succeed, and fail, but you didn't give up. You reached your hand out to the Lord for help and I saw Him respond with miracle after miracle, fortifying my faith at the same time. The girls and I remember listening when you gave your testimony at church for the first time, and then sat amazed by the response of so many men, teens, and families who came forward who have been struggling with the same issue and were praying for help. It is truly an honor to see you use your gifts for the Lord once more, something that so many were quick to forever disqualify you from ever doing again. But this time it's different. You are free and open, empathetic and at peace, and connected in a sacred relationship with your Heavenly Father.

It has been a long road, my love, but we are overcomers in Christ Jesus. You and I are overcomers. I love the love we share and new life we are building and living. You are my armor bearer and I am yours. It fills me with inexplicable joy to think of sharing the remaining days of my life with you.

You are my forever love,
Teri

OUR PASTOR'S ADMONISHMENT AND BLESSING

VOWS

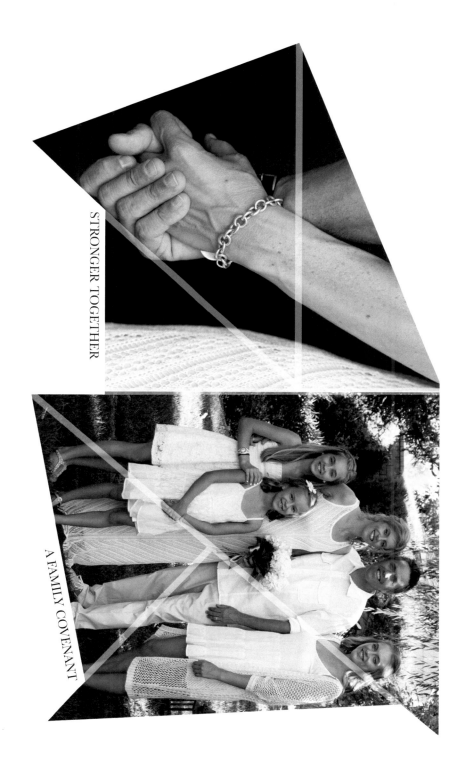

STRONGER TOGETHER

A FAMILY COVENANT

BOUND TOGETHER IN CHRIST

If you are receiving this invitation, it is because you have played a significant part in our family's restoration.

Whether your divine function was through prayer, support, accountability, or you literally got into the trenches with us as we battled for our future, we couldn't have made it without you.

It is with great love and gratitude that we stand before you in the presence of the Lord and renew our covenant with one another in unity and solidarity.

We believe this important act will not only spiritually bind us together in Christ, but also bring generational harmony to our beloved daughters and their children to come.

It is no small matter to walk with a person in the darkest hours of their life.

The great love and kindness you have bestowed upon our family will be remembered forever.

The pleasure of your company is requested
At the celebration of the
Covenant Renewal between

TERI
&
JAMES

Saturday, the sixteenth of August
Two thousand and fourteen

CELEBRATING MARRIAGE, SUMMER 2014

FAMILY SURF DAY, SUMMER 2014

BAPTISM INTO OUR NEW LIFE, JUNE 2014

RAINY WINTER WALK WITH OUR DOG FIGGY

SPRING 2014
SUNSET AND SISTERS IN MALIBU

CRAFT FAMILY CHRISTMAS CARD PICTURE, 2013

SUMMER 2013
HIKING IN MAMMOTH

FAMILY FUN W/ GRANDMA
SUMMER 2013

OUR EBENEZER STONE

A LIVING STONE

I am a common Commodity,
Like a weathered and worn stone,
Whose edges have been softened
By the winds and storms of life.

But I have been preserved for such a time as this,
As a reminder and a monument
Of the One who formed my heart.

And though I may find myself
Adrift on a distant and remote shore,
I will not fear,
knowing I am never out of Your reach.

For it is You who calls my name,
And You who leads me on.

Teri Craft
written May 2013

OUR FAVORITE WALKING SPOT—WAIMANALO, MAY 2013